THE IMPORTANCE OF BEING BARBRA

THE IMPORTANCE OF BEING

Barbra

TOM SANTOPIETRO

THOMAS DUNNE BOOKS ST. MARTIN'S PRESS ✠ NEW YORK

THOMAS DUNNE BOOKS.
An imprint of St. Martin's Press.

www.stmartins.com

Library of Congress Cataloging-in-Publication Data

Santopietro, Tom.
    The importance of being Barbra / Tom Santopietro.
        p. cm
    Includes bibliographical references.
    ISBN 0-312-34879-7
    EAN 978-0-312-34879-3
        1. Streisand, Barbra.   2. Singers—United States—Biography.   I. Title.
    ML420.S915336 2006
    782.42164092—dc22

                                                                2006040197

First Edition: June 2006

10   9   8   7   6   5   4   3   2   1

For Mom and Dad
The Best of the Greatest Generation

Contents

Acknowledgments

Special thanks to Mark Erickson, who first read the manuscript, to Alan Markinson for the tapes and quips, to Peter Joseph at St. Martin's Press for his good-natured and thorough assistance, and to my editor, Tom Dunne, for his judgment and guidance.

Preface

April 14, 1969: Twenty-six-year-old Barbra Streisand nervously sits in her aisle seat—with recently separated husband Elliott Gould by her side for moral support—as Ingrid Bergman reads the names of the five nominees for Best Actress in a Motion Picture at the 41st Annual Academy Awards ceremony: Katharine Hepburn—*The Lion in Winter,* Patricia Neal—*The Subject Was Roses,* Vanessa Redgrave—*Isadora,* Barbra Streisand—*Funny Girl,* and Joanne Woodward—*Rachel, Rachel.* Bergman unseals the envelope, intoning "The winner . . . ," then gasps. "It's a tie! The winners are—Katharine Hepburn in *The Lion in Winter*—and Barbra Streisand!" Hepburn, the Hollywood legend, absent as always from awards shows, is nowhere to be seen. Hollywood newcomer Streisand, already an entertainment legend, albeit of a very different stripe, and now an Oscar winner for her very first film, rises from her seat, and after the surprise of the tie, a second shock ensues for the audience: Barbra's Scaasi-designed pantsuit ensemble is nothing less than see-through. In her excitement and haste, Barbra stumbles up the stairs to the strains of "People" as she approaches the stage to receive her award, thereby exposing even more of the Streisand physiognomy to the tens of millions watching worldwide. It's as if everyone has the exact same thought at the exact same time: "Does she have anything on underneath?"

Upon receiving the actual statue, Streisand gazes at her Oscar and in a witty echo of her character-defining first line in *Funny Girl,* jokes, "Hello, gorgeous!" Of course, the line has been planned, but in her winning delivery it works; the audience laughs warmly and is with her all the way. Thinking fast on her feet, the Brooklyn-born neophyte gracefully compliments WASP icon Hepburn: "I'm very honored to be in such magnificent company as Katharine Hepburn." Following Bergman offstage, Barbra clutches her Oscar, and when she meets the press, flashbulbs pop, hundreds of photos are snapped, and the very next day, newspaper readers around the world are staring at Hollywood's newest star in her much-talked-about, much-dissected see-through designer outfit. And, by the way, she's holding her Oscar.

Nearly forty years later, people remember that Barbra won the Oscar, and definitely remember the outfit—a state of affairs which provides a neat snapshot of the dichotomy at the heart of so much of the Streisand career. Even when Barbra was a mere twenty-six, the work—oftentimes dazzling, occasionally inexplicable—was filtered through reactions to her dress, her bluntness, her personal life—in short to the personality as outsized as her talent. It was this inability of others to separate the personal from the professional, their inability to review the work itself and not her relentless search for perfection, that rankled La Streisand (having earned, or rather been saddled with, that appellation at the age of twenty-two while starring in *Funny Girl* on Broadway). Yes, she sure as hell wanted the awards and the approbation of her peers, but having conquered every area of show business while still a youngster—turning thirty with an Oscar, Tony, Emmys, and Grammys in hand—she was, perhaps understandably, seemingly deflated to discover the full extent of the American dream's underside: the sniping, schadenfreude, and constant prying into her personal life.

Were the successes enough to offset this ongoing, oftentimes relentless public scrutiny? On the plus side of the ledger, the statistics are downright gaudy, and for sheer range are unparalleled in the history of show business: one Tony Award, two Oscars, six Emmys, eight Grammys, ten Golden Globes, thirteen multi-platinum, thirty-one platinum albums, fifty gold records, the best-selling pop female vocalist of all time, the American Film Institute's Life Achievement Award—it's a list downright exhausting to contemplate in its entirety. Couple this with a public persona that embodies the Cinderella myth—ugly duckling turned swan who conquers Broadway, television, recordings, Hollywood, in short nothing less than the entire entertainment universe (or is it the entire universe?), only to find true love with handsome real-life Prince Charming, James Brolin, as she nears age sixty—and it's the stuff of legend, an improbably full-blown Technicolor Hollywood musical come to life.

This is success of unprecedented scope, the stuff of dreams, but it has come at a terrible cost. As the first version of *A Star Is Born* asked in its very title, "What Price Hollywood?" Always a pertinent question, the query takes on additional meaning in the case of Barbra Streisand, for the result of Barbra fulfilling every last one of her childhood dreams is that she has lost all semblance of a normal private life. Ironically, unlike many stars who publicly profess their desire for privacy, but seem to wilt when away from the spotlight, Barbra genuinely craves that privacy, an outgrowth of her basically shy personality. Attempting to maintain this privacy, she granted virtually no interviews once ensconced as the Queen of Hollywood, a status achieved by 1969 (a mere eight years after beginning her professional career). Work in live theatre ceased and concerts became a distant memory. Any semblance of live contact with the public evaporated, Barbra being much more comfortable in recording studios or on movie sets, environments where total control could be exercised. Yet rather than driving her public away, such actions only increased Barbra's allure. Streisand fans were just that—fanatical—and many secretly thrilled to her seeming hauteur. No attempt at just-folks here—this was a diva, in all senses of the word. In Barbra's case, make that überdiva—no one else came close to matching her talent, drive, money, prestige, awards, controversy, and most significantly, power.

But—and it's a very big but—even her most impassioned fans misread the Streisand attitude. She didn't disdain her fans, which is how many interpreted her aloof behavior; in fact, she was appreciative of their support, as she noted in the *Streisand Superman* liner notes, written following the critical drubbing she received on *A Star Is Born*. She just wanted the fans to focus on the work, not on her private life, and she genuinely didn't seem to understand the fans' worship that dovetailed with her public persona, as it does with all divas. Uncomfortable with the adulation of these most obsessive fans, her public pronouncements all but told them, "Thank you for your support, but please—get a life of your own."

The interesting contradiction at the heart of Barbra Streisand's public life is that her high-profile professional projects, coupled with her unwavering determination to voice her political opinions, guarantee the one thing she doesn't want: that every aspect of her life will continue to be put under the microscope. In the celebrity-obsessed world of 2005, a world which seemed to begin with the mid-1970s debut of *People* magazine, this is and will remain a part of the equation for public life. To a certain degree, Barbra Streisand, a very savvy participant in the celebrity sweepstakes, understands this. The contradiction actually lies in the fact that even after forty-plus years in the spotlight, Barbra Streisand remains remarkably thin-skinned, seemingly unable to forget even the slightest criticism. For better and worse, she cares, and as with everything in her life, cares with unbridled passion. It's why she remains so extraordinarily successful, and why the process still seems to prove so painful for her. Even cosseted away in her hilltop Malibu mansion, surrounded by manicured gardens and bathed in sunshine, light-years away from the relentless streets of her native Brooklyn—living indeed in a setting designed, dressed, and lit by the diva herself—she cannot fully escape. That, the subtext of her public pronouncements seems to say, is not what she bargained for.

This yin/yang pull between the public and the private has manifested itself more strongly with Streisand than with almost any other entertainment figure (Garbo flat-out retired and Katharine Hepburn actually grew increasingly accessible through the years), for Barbra Streisand remains a walking mass of contradictions, a state of affairs which plays no small part in her worldwide iconic status. The fast-talking funny girl speaking pure Brooklynese has become a woman of surpassing seriousness, more interested in political pronouncements than light entertainment. In the 1960s, her personality, appearance, and outlook blazed a new trail, but even as the rock revolution engulfed the entire music scene, Barbra's true artistry and musical soul lay firmly in an exploration of the past—the great American songbook of the previous four decades. Obsessive in her work, relentless in her attention to detail, she loves the craft of making movies, but her all-consuming perfectionism proves so exhausting to her that in the last twenty-seven years, she has made only six films. The greatest theatrical singer of her generation—arguably the greatest ever—she has been so paralyzed by stage fright that from 1967 through 2005, she undertook exactly one concert tour. A so-called ugly duckling turned swan, hailed as both weirdo and great beauty, she helped change an entire nation's notion of beauty, yet continues to publicly work out her insecurity about physical appearance by means of multi-million-dollar films. A steely one-woman entertainment industry who successfully forged her own path as actress, singer, producer, and director in the until recently overwhelmingly male-dominated world of Hollywood, she can still display an almost palpable sense of vulnerability in flashes of her film work. Willing to battle any and all obstacles en route to achieving her professional goals, she remains extraordinarily shy in social settings. Who would have thunk it, but there must be days when it's exhausting and just plain tough to be Barbra Streisand.

Jazz legend Dizzy Gillespie once cannily remarked, "The professional is the guy who can do it twice." Given the depth and scope of Streisand's achievements, by the standards of this aphorism Barbra

Streisand qualifies as the ultimate professional. And, if that she is, then after all these years, what do the professional achievements look like when stripped of the distorting prism of any personal overlay? Stripped of biographical adornment, what does a case-by-case examination of the work itself reveal?

When Streisand opened her landmark *The Broadway Album* with Stephen Sondheim's "Putting It Together," that dazzling song about the creative process featured a partially revamped lyric, custom-tailored to the Streisand specifications. As with the vast majority of the Streisand oeuvre, there existed an iron-willed reason behind it all: Behind the album-opening placement of the song, behind the special lyric, and especially behind her intensely personal connection to the song—she was singing about her life's work, damn it.

> *Art isn't easy,*
> *Every minor detail is a major decision.*

Streisand and Sondheim: Notorious perfectionists both. She— intuitive and smart. He—highly educated and cerebral. Both obsessive in their attention to detail, attention that fuels their art.

> *Have to keep things in scale*
> *Have to hold to your vision—*

Sondheim on Streisand: "Her work is exactly what 'Putting It Together' is about. She works the way Seurat worked on his painting, dot by dot, moment by moment, bar by bar and note by note. . . . The only thing that surprised me was that she paid as much exquisite attention to detail in the orchestration as she did in her own singing. . . . That's why it's so good. It's not just the gift, it's the willingness to take infinite pains."

Be new, girl
They tell you till they're blue, girl
You're new or else you're through, girl
And even if it's true, girl
You do what you can do. . . .

Sondheim's right on the money with his words and music, as is Streisand in her interpretation. In single-minded pursuit of their vision, both are artists who blaze new trails and inevitably court controversy. But in Streisand's case, over the years the groundbreaking work could meander onto overly safe paths, the choices framed by a blinkered vision that proved downright difficult to fathom. Which leaves the key question: When was her work indeed art, and when was it a waste of an extraordinary, once in a lifetime, talent?

June 1994

Fifteen thousand strong, rising for the fifth—or was it the sixth?—standing ovation of the evening, the Madison Square Garden crowd yelled out their song requests to fifty-two-year-old Barbra Streisand as she stood quietly in the spotlight. An almost pleasant sense of desperation pervaded the crowd on this warm June night in 1994, desperation born of a fear that this rare live connection with their idol would evaporate before they told her which song she *had* to sing for them. Twenty-seven years they had waited while Barbra Joan Streisand pursued her perfectionist vision in the totally controlled environs of recording studios and sound stages. Twenty-seven years since the last public concert in New York City, the fabled "Happening in Central Park." Never mind that the 1967 Central Park concert was free, and that tickets to "The Concert," as this Madison Square Garden happening was modestly entitled, cost up to $350 per ticket—and much more than that from the myriad scalpers who delighted in their record business. None of that mattered to the ardent fans who had waited to tell their hometown girl how much they loved her. How much she meant to them. It was quite a sight as this upscale, upper-middle-class—hell—upper-middle-aged crowd shed decorum and screamed out their requests. " 'Stoney End, Barbra! Sing 'Second Hand Rose'!" And as the requests multiplied, Barbra Streisand did something most unexpected; for the first time all evening she looked away from the TelePrompTer, which scrolled every word she would utter in this record-breaking triumphant return. Smiling quizzically at the adoring crowd, she cracked wise: "You know, I have this all planned out."

Did she ever.

Beginnings

And I want to be famous. I don't care whether it's by singing or acting or what, I want everybody to know my name, even the cowboys!

—Barbra Streisand, *Seventeen,* October 1963

She was a skinny flibbertigibbet with no discipline and no technique. . . . All she had was this enormous talent.

—Producer David Merrick on the young, pre-*I Can Get It For You Wholesale* Barbra Streisand, *Saturday Evening Post,* July 27, 1963

She's made life a lot better for a helluva lot of homely girls.

—Isobel Lennart,

Bookwriter/Screenwriter, *Funny Girl*

When Barbra Joan Streisand, Brooklyn, New York native, Erasmus Hall High School grad, arrived on the scene in 1960, New York City was a different country. Hell, America was a different country. For a trip downtown in anytown USA, women dressed in hats and gloves. It was the era of the man in the gray flannel suit and the three-martini executive lunch. In Vegas the Rat Pack held sway, while in New York City the leading hotels maintained elegant supper clubs where Ella Fitzgerald, Lena Horne, and Tony Bennett performed. The rock-and-roll revolution which Elvis Presley jump-started may have grown increasingly powerful, but original cast albums of Broadway shows still hit the record charts—*Camelot* and *Bye Bye Birdie* could still generate airplay. The era of the great American songbook was entering the final flowering of its golden era.

The seemingly quiescent Eisenhower years were similarly drifting to an end. Fathers worked, mothers stayed at home, families contained 2.4 children and 1 dog, and minorities, restive through the beginnings of the civil rights era, still largely "knew their place." Homosexuals—invisible. Cancer—literally whispered about. Divorce—a shock. Turmoil may have roiled the waters beneath the placid surface, but on top, all remained calm.

WASPs ruled American society, but the second generation of im-

migrants from Europe, those born in the U.S. in the twenties and thir-
ties, were increasingly staking their claim to a piece of the mythic
American dream. These were the new doctors and lawyers with the
increased economic clout that accompanied their new positions. The
economic order was rearranging itself with increasing rapidity, but
the societal pecking order? Italians and Jews may have been chiefs of
surgery at their hospitals, but only now, in 1960, were the Italians—
not the Jews—allowed to join the WASPy enclave of the country-club
world. A country-club world where couples foxtrotted to the soothing sounds of a bland combo, throwing in a cha-cha or mambo on
"South of the Border" night. New York City jazz clubs may have
showcased the avant-garde, but the stereos at home—featuring the
modern hi-fi sound—those were stocked with Rosemary Clooney,
Ella Fitzgerald, and the music of the number one box office attraction
in the country: Doris Day.

Perky, pretty, even sexy in a wholesome way, Doris Day could sing
in a surprisingly seductive, intimate manner; languid ballads like "Stars
Fell on Alabama" and "Sleepy Lagoon" spoke of late-night ren-
dezvous, but on the surface it was the lingering echo of the big band
music and ethos of the World War II generation who had fully as-
sumed control of the country with the election of JFK. Doris Day
personified the sound of confident, hands-on-hips, post-WWII America. Roll up the sleeves, tackle the problem head on—she was the girl
you wanted to bring home to mother. Corn-fed and definitely Mid-
western. Which was everything eighteen-year-old Barbra Streisand
most definitely was not.

In the America of July 1960, to a surprisingly large extent, even in
New York City, everyone was trying to be the same American. Such
attempts were doomed to failure of course, but the effort was being
made, even by those who didn't particularly want to do so. But Barbra
Streisand couldn't conceive of even making the effort—a startling

frame of mind for an unknown, strange-looking eighteen-year-old girl, especially in 1960.

This individualistic frame of mind was to immediately endear Barbra to outcasts of all stripes across America. Why, Barbra seemed to reason, should she try to fit in? She wanted to stand out, not live like everyone else. It was, in the Barbra lexicon, not only impossible for her to blend in, but a waste of time to even try, and this was one girl who had no time to spare. Barbra Streisand thought fast, she walked fast, and boy oh boy did she ever talk fast, with a thick Brooklyn accent and machine-gun rapid patter.

Well, her reasoning seemed to run, with her looks how could she ever fit in? True, her looks were different, but ironically, the ugly-duckling myth that instantly sprang up around Streisand, oftentimes propelled forward by Barbra herself, obscured one very important fact: Barbra Streisand was never ugly. Unusual-looking—yes. Gawky—sure. Homely—on occasion. (Barbra herself laughed at her adolescent visage—complete with corsage—when a photo of her teenaged self was flashed onscreen during the triumphant 1994 concerts. Quipped the diva: "Some things improve with age.")

I kept my nose to spite my face.
—Stephen Sondheim's new lyric to "I'm Still Here,"
as sung by Streisand in her 1994 concert tour

But—and it's a very big but—Barbra Streisand was always striking. Look at the pictures throughout the years: the photo of little Barbara Joan on the cover of the *My Name is Barbra* album—that's a cute, skinny little girl. The nose which dominates her face is actually fascinating to look at, and photographs beautifully. If anything, one wants to touch the nose—feel the bump and planes. It's really the eyes that jar, being both small and set close together. Even there, however, the eyes are so blue that the viewer is captivated. Finally, Barbra Streisand possessed one further, not so incidental attribute: Even as an eighteen-year-old girl, she was highly sensual. The slender frame, the mixture of steel and vulnerability, the willowy hands and all-enveloping voice—like any real star, Barbra Streisand carried a sexual charge. It just came in a package unlike any ever previously glimpsed.

Through the years, personalities as diverse as Phyllis Diller and Orson Bean have claimed that *they* were the ones who told Barbra not to have a nose job. Maybe Streisand herself was afraid a nose job would affect her voice. Who knows? What matters is that even at age eighteen, when self-perceptions of beauty are at their most heightened—especially for those in show business—Barbra instinctively knew that she'd be compromising herself, compromising her very integrity, if she submitted to the surgery. In effect, by refusing to alter her nose, Streisand refused assimilation and proudly asserted her Jewishness. This was no easy feat in the America of 1960, and it is a decision that has resonated with her fans throughout the ensuing decades.

Unlike the hugely popular Doris Day, even in 1960 the eighteen-year-old Barbra Joan Streisand could never conceive of singing "Que Sera, Sera": She'd make things happen—no placid acceptance of whatever will be, will be for her. There would certainly be no following the traditional show business paths of her elders. It's not as if this questioning of traditions and authority started at age eighteen, or even at age thirteen when she argued with/directed the pianist at the "recording session" where she and her mother recorded demos. This was a girl who questioned and dared authority in all its guises and clearly had done so from the time she could walk and talk. Musing about herself as a little girl, Barbra noted, "When the rabbi would go out of the room (at the Brooklyn Yeshiva I attended until third grade), I'd yell 'Christmas! Christmas!'—a bad word for Hebrew school." If it took the unorthodox strategy of entering a talent contest at a Greenwich Village gay bar—the Lion—to jump-start her career, then that's exactly what she'd do. And did. She wanted to be noticed, and the start of that journey would be facing down the hypercritical gay audience at the Lion, an audience that recognized the first notes of "A Sleepin' Bee" as the elegant, beautiful Diahann Carroll's signature song from Harold Arlen and Truman Capote's *House of Flowers*. Strangely riveted by this skinny girl in her antique T-strap shoes, the audience waited. To pounce.

Which they never did. After the final lyric of "My one true love I has found," words sung with crystal-clear diction and extraordinary purity, utter silence fell on the room. The ovation in that tiny room began to swell and it was Ella Fitzgerald winning the Apollo Theater's Amateur Night contest all over again. Destiny pure and simple. Barbra Joan Streisand was on her way.

In fact, the myth surrounding the start of her career holds that Barbra Streisand arrived a perfectly formed artist, sui generis. Obscured is the fact that Barry Dennen, California native and actor, later to obtain some fame as Pontius Pilate in the original Broadway production of *Jesus Christ Superstar,* helped prepare Streisand's arrangements of "A Sleepin' Bee" and "Lover Come Back To Me." THAT VOICE—and it was always THAT VOICE in capital letters—was hers, of course. But at the beginning, the interpretations were worked out with the help of Dennen (who became her first boyfriend, as well). Dennen introduced her to famous female vocalists of the twentieth century—Ruth Etting, Lee Wiley, Mabel Mercer—and Streisand soaked up every lesson, hungering for more, driving towards the stardom she *knew* awaited her.

The Lion led to an audition for the Bon Soir nightclub on Eighth Street, and the important addition of Peter Daniels as her accompanist. Impressed with the musicality she displayed at the William Morris Agency audition where he had accompanied her, Daniels played for her audition at the Bon Soir, one she passed with flying colors.

At the Bon Soir, Barbra Streisand, singer—file and forget.
—Rogers Whitaker's *New Yorker* review of
Streisand's nightclub appearance

That old fart! What does he know?
—Unknown 18-year-old Barbra Streisand's response to the review

Continuing to work with both Dennen and Daniels, Barbra refined gestures and reconsidered vocal inflections; the extraordinary attention to detail had begun, and word began to circulate about the strange-looking girl with the very strange antique clothes, singing odd songs like 'Who's Afraid of the Big Bad Wolf'—in a breathtaking voice.

A small obsessive claque of fans began to attend many of her twice-nightly sets of five songs at the Bon Soir. Fascinated patrons would ask to buy her a drink; she asked instead for a baked potato with "hard crust and extra butter." The word grew: This girl was talented and a complete kook. Who asked for a baked potato instead of a drink?! It was also at the Bon Soir that two important constants of Streisand's professional life began to take shape: the need for her mother's approval and the presence of a very devoted gay following.

Attending her daughter's second-night performance, Diana Streisand Kind was, in Barbra's own words, "totally embarrassed by me. She thought I was singing in my underwear!"—not the Victorian-era white lace combing jacket that Barbra combined with a self-designed skirt. The outfit may seem quaint now, but in the buttoned-down world of 1962, no one, but no one, wore an outfit like this while singing in a nightclub. This girl was an original, but it wasn't an originality of appearance appreciated by her own mother. Apparently, criticism was offered of Barbra's clothes but no positive comment was made about her performance. Mrs. Kind didn't want her daughter to "get a swelled head," so praise was not forthcoming; the comments that were made, however, remained imprinted upon Barbra's memory even decades later: "When I was eighteen, I sang at the Bon Soir and when my mother came to see me her comment was, 'Your voice is very thin. You need eggs in your milk to make your voice stronger' . . ." Pressed for praise of any sort, Mrs. Kind is supposed to have simply stated, "You did good." This comment was poignantly echoed thirty-four years later when *Vanity Fair* writer Michael Shnayerson overheard Diana telling Barbra "somewhat grudgingly—'You did good. I'm proud of you,'" after one of Barbra's record-breaking performances before fifteen thousand screaming fans at Anaheim's Pond Center. It was only then, in 1994, that the fifty-two-year-old Barbra was actually able to state that she and her mother "get along better now. We're able to say 'I love you' to each other . . . She showed her love through food, rather than hugs and kisses."

The key is that for the young Barbra, the lifelong pattern of needing her mother's approval had simply moved from the personal into the arena of professional achievement. If Diana didn't notice her at home (pretty, younger half sister Roslyn Kind occupying most of Diana's time in Barbra's view), then Barbra would be doubly sure to make Diana notice her onstage. Look at ME. Ruminating on her eighteen-year-old self from the vantage point of 1991, Barbra neatly, if somewhat painfully, summarized her mother's role in fueling her overwhelming ambition: "But by her not understanding me she's responsible for my success. I had to prove to my mother that you don't have to be beautiful to be a movie star . . . Now I look at her with enormous gratitude and I can feel love. I have no more anger . . . I lived for many years with a lot of anger at my parents."

And while Diana withheld any effusive praise, the gay fans who were to become Barbra's most fervent admirers, even at this early stage of her career, began to follow her every move. If the gay audience's identification with Judy Garland was born at best out of a shared sense of vulnerability, and at worst out of a shared sense of misery—a sense of the fantasy life over the rainbow in those pre-Stonewall days—then the identification with Barbra twenty years later was one of mutual outsider status. Mocked for outward appearance, Barbra and her gay fans shared the trait of being marginalized. Just as the gay community struggled to take its first steps living life out of the closet, Barbra simply demanded to be included amongst those in control. The show-business establishment wouldn't accept her on their terms? Fine—she'd break the rules and make new ones, and her gay audience, always keen to discover new talent, was ready to go along for the ride. The time was not yet ripe for Madonna and her gay fans' fuck-you attitude towards the establishment—that would follow twenty years later. Instead, Barbra played on her outsider status, thereby ensuring permanent identification from anyone ever left eating lunch by themselves at school.

What Streisand herself knew, even at this early stage, was that it should always be about the music. She thought of herself as an actress—okay, an actress who sings—but she cannily realized that her voice would open doors otherwise closed to her. The talent contest at the Lion led to the eleven-week engagement at the Bon Soir, which led to *I Can Get It For You Wholesale,* which led to *Funny Girl,* which led to Hollywood and legend time, but it started with THAT VOICE, and with the two men who helped shape her musical direction: Peter Daniels and arranger Peter Matz.

The importance of the roles played by the two Peters cannot be overstated. Peter Daniels picked up where Barry Dennen had left off. Daniels, who later married Streisand's *Funny Girl* understudy Lainie Kazan, was overwhelmed by Streisand's voice. She in turn greatly respected his musical knowledge and listened to his musical advice; if Dennen still had some say in choice of material and order of performance, Daniels suggested tempos, inflections, and pacing. Harold

Arlen, an early fan of Streisand's whose works featured prominently on the first albums, then introduced Streisand to Peter Matz, and the missing link for a successful recording career was in place: the arranger.

Matz came to occupy the role for Streisand that Nelson Riddle filled with Sinatra: Like Riddle, Matz was an immensely talented arranger who intuitively understood what showcased the star to best advantage. Streisand, like Bing Crosby before her, possessed a voice made for the microphone, creating an intimacy with the listener on ballads and a warm, enveloping sound on up-tempo numbers. Matz knew just how to capitalize on this sound—when to emphasize the brass for her "belt" voice and when to float the vocal on a cushion of strings. Matz understood her in a way no one has since. It is no accident that the best of her early work—*The Second Barbra Streisand Album* and *The Third Album*—were overseen by Matz, just as the best CD from the second twenty years of her recording career, *The Broadway Album*, reunited her with Matz for the first time in over a decade.

With the addition of Matz, all of the components were in place for Barbra's first recording: a supremely talented vocalist, a terrific arranger and conductor, and in Columbia Records, a major label with the resources to promote the finished product. One burning question remained: Was there a mass audience for the very different looking and sounding Barbra Streisand outside of the rarified atmosphere of Manhattan nightclubs? The answer came through loud and clear immediately upon release of her very first album.

Recordings

Streisand is tempermental. She's got her own ideas about music and she's not happy unless it's done exactly the way she wants. I only did a couple of sessions with her because I found her so difficult to work with, but then, so does everybody else.'

—violinist Dave Frisina as quoted in Will Friedwald's *Sinatra! The Song Is You: A Singer's Art*

The producers wish to extend their deepest thanks and gratitude . . . to Barbra Streisand . . . the most gracious and gifted talent we have ever known.'

—Rupert Holmes and Jeffrey Lesser, producers of Barbra Streisand's *Lazy Afternoon* album

When *The Barbra Streisand Album* was released in 1963 (after Barbra's cameo vocal appearances on cast recordings of *Pins and Needles* and *I Can Get It For You Wholesale*), it became an unexpected smash hit, rising to the top of the charts and, incredibly enough, winning a Grammy as album of the year. It was an incredible win simply because the album is wildly uneven, a fact that appears to have been overlooked in the collective joy of having a new kind of dream girl on the scene. The breathtaking, youthful beauty of "Soon It's Gonna Rain," sung in a voice pure enough to silence an entire room of listeners, is offset by an over-the-top version of "Cry Me a River" featuring an out-of-control Streisand screaming her heartache about the lover who has deserted her. There is no sense of proportion to the recording; for every haunting "A Sleepin' Bee," there is a self-conscious "Come to the Supermarket."

Why then did the album become a hit? Why, in short, did it resonate with the audience?

It worked for two solid reasons. First, the good cuts were sensational, filled with a startling urgency that was new for audiences accustomed to the soothing style of Jo Stafford and Dinah Shore. Barbra Streisand sang as if her life depended on it, and whether you liked her or not, you could not *not* pay attention.

Second, it wasn't just the purity of her voice that riveted the listener. It was the fact that in her personal life, as well as in song choice, she embodied yearning, the search for all of life's possibilities. The combination of voice and song choice with the ugly duckling/Cinderella myth which she personified, embellished, and sometimes wielded as a weapon resulted very quickly in Streisand's fan base exploding beyond the big cities where she first became popular. That voice the microphone loved, riding the waves of a surging orchestra or seamlessly negotiating the trickiest of rhythms—it all created an intimacy with her listeners across the country. The unloved, unattractive girls in small-town America identified with the fact that Barbra Streisand was definitely not the wholesome, pretty girl next door. She had a large nose and sported bizarre outfits like the one in *The Barbra Streisand Album*'s cover shot: a herringbone vest covering her Peter Pan–collared blouse. The boys ridiculed as hopeless outcasts, or worst of all gay, the adults afraid that life would pass them by—they all identified with Streisand's quest to knock down every obstacle in her way. If Barbra plowed right through those who had called her too ugly, too weird, too Jewish, too loud, too too too everything, well then maybe, just maybe, her fans could timidly knock on some of those closed doors themselves. "Hey," their reasoning ran, "she's a misfit. The kids in school called her names too—'big beak,' 'crazy Barbra'—and her mother didn't pay attention to her either. But she's still making it. I *want* her to make it. Big."

A sense of identification was born, and as Barbra began publicly telling the stories of her miserable childhood every chance she had, one could almost see and hear her ever-growing number of fans increasing their obsessive identification with her. Over the years, no matter how grand or remote Barbra became as she hid herself away as the Queen of Hollywood, that core connection was never broken. As Stephen Holden wrote in his *Rolling Stone* review of *Barbra Joan Streisand,* "The high point of the album, the Bacharach-David medley (of "One Less Bell to Answer"/"A House Is Not a Home"), is pure vintage Streisand. A duet with herself, she croons it like it is for all the male models and Marjorie Morningstars of the world with klieg lights in their eyes."

After this uneven, albeit oftentimes exciting, debut album, it is startling then to hear the quantum leap present in *The Second Barbra Streisand Album*. Recorded in 1963, and replete with Harold Arlen classics, this is the work of a fully mature, seasoned performer. "Any Place I Hang My Hat Is Home" is sung with a sexuality that tells you that this girl has been around the block. "When the Sun Comes Out" may be a torch song about the end of *her* world, but she is in control every step of the way. "Who Will Buy?" from the Broadway musical *Oliver!* is sung with the heartbreaking naiveté of a girl searching for the life over the rainbow; the range is astonishing and in only her second recording, Streisand is in full cry, cushioned by the canny arrangements and conducting of Peter Matz.

Displaying a range of moods rivaled only by Judy Garland in her prime, Barbra hit upon another element to cement the growing legend: the liner notes. The liner notes on her first album were written by no less a musical legend than Harold Arlen, who advised the public to "Watch, listen, and remember: I told you so." On *The Second Barbra Streisand Album,* liner notes by Jule Styne, of *Gypsy* and Hollywood musical fame, reinforced the obvious evidence that here was an actress, an actress who made every song into a three-act play. In all his years of writing songs and being associated with top singers, Jule Styne had "never been as thrilled as he was listening to this new album." These were words Streisand liked. She'd show them. She'd show the world.

Which she did, and then some, with the release of *The Third Album*. Ten classic pop songs, ranging from "Betwitched, Bothered and Bewildered" through "Just in Time" to "I Had Myself a True Love." Included therein: arguably the definitive version of "As Time Goes By." Cover photo by Roddy McDowall. Liner notes by Oscar-winning lyricist Sammy Cahn. Working with the very best arrangers and con-

REHEARSAL FOR A 1963 RECORDING SESSION. *PHOTOFEST*

ductors in the business: Ray Ellis, Sid Ramin, Peter Matz. Nary a false note or misplaced emphasis. Great popular singing on time-tested standards, drawing the listener through no less than the full cycle of love: yearning, passion, betrayal, longing, and hope. All this at age twenty-two.

With the release of *The Third Album,* the very nature of Barbra Streisand's appeal had become clear: She possessed an unequalled ability to convey both the hurt of lost love and a burning desire so intense that it struck at the very core of the listener's being. At times the intensity of the attack was downright eerie, as if the fate of Western civilization hung in the balance as she sang of her lost love. It all rang true because Barbra Streisand was not pretending, and the public intuitively understood that fact. These early recordings and live appearances provided nothing short of a desperately needed outlet for the intense feelings of loneliness, of otherness, that seemed to pour out of her. If the sound of Frank Sinatra's voice evoked the lonely urban male, bruised by love, sitting at the end of the bar nursing scotch and regret, Streisand summoned up lost love of a different sort, and there was nothing musing about it at all. Her voice conveyed yearning and a world of "if onlys": "If only he knew the real me, if only I had a chance. Where's my Prince Charming?" The entire equation, in fact, was to be beautifully revealed on her *My Name Is Barbra, Two* . . . LP when she lit into the Rodgers and Hart standard "Where's That Rainbow?" and laid out the whole damn shooting match in exactly three minutes and thirty-seven seconds.

After the triumph of *The Third Album,* four more recordings were released in the short space of eighteen months. The result? Four home runs in a row. First up—the 1964 Capitol Records *Funny Girl* cast recording. In a climate where Broadway cast albums no longer led the sales charts, the *Funny Girl* LP rose all the way to #2 on the *Billboard* listings, based solely upon the appeal of Barbra Streisand. It's a totally understandable success because the recording is, in a word, sensational. For once, the excitement of a live Broadway show is captured on disc.

It's not just the size of Barbra's vocal role as Fanny Brice: seven solos, two duets, three production numbers. It's not just the realization that Barbra belted out this marathon role eight times per week for nearly two years on Broadway. It's that composer Jule Styne clearly wrote the score with the Streisand voice in mind (just as he wrote *Gypsy* with Merman's clarion voice in his head) and in tandem with lyricist Bob Merrill gave her no fewer than four eleven-o'clock—i.e., wrap-it-up-and-send-'em-home—numbers, all of which she handled beautifully. Barbra runs the gamut from exuberant "I am" songs— "I'm the Greatest Star"—to dramatic ballads—"People"—to razzle-dazzle belters—"Don't Rain On My Parade"—and she never misses a note, literally or figuratively. In charting the life of Fanny Brice, Barbra develops a fully realized human being, which is not only a real accomplishment in the often cartoonish world of Broadway musicals, but particularly extraordinary when one realizes that she has accomplished this on record simply by means of her voice.

In a disc of continuous highlights, best of all is the penultimate number in the score, the lovely "The Music That Makes Me Dance." Cushioned by the enveloping sound of Ralph Burns's string-laden orchestration, it's a lost-love song par excellence, delivered by *the* ballad singer of her time, and every bit as good as the "My Man" finale to the *Funny Girl* film. Listening to the disc forty years after its original release is to be reminded again of how extraordinary Barbra was at the very young age of twenty-two.

It is interesting to compare the twenty-two-year-old Barbra with Johnny Mathis, a singer she had listened to and admired as a youngster, and one who also personifies yearning, albeit from the male perspective. This synchronicity made their 1993 *Back to Broadway* duet on the Leonard Bernstein/Stephen Sondheim *West Side Story* classics "I Have a Love/One Hand, One Heart" especially effective. After all, in the most basic terms, what show dealt more with yearning than *West Side Story?* But Mathis's emotions remained closed—paralyzingly shy on stage, he barely spoke to the audience, simply presenting his voice as an object of beauty, a gift to be shared, but done so remotely. All of the emotions had to be provided by the listener. Streisand, with the same purity of tone, the same miles of vocal chords, attacked from the other end of the spectrum. She was an actress, damn it, and the world would know not just what character she was portraying, but how she, Barbra, felt. It was in-your-face theatrics, all-out attack, and at this point in her career, most people thrilled to the sound.

Capitalizing on the success of Barbra's hit single signature recording of "People," Columbia Records released another solo album in 1964 entitled *People*. Her third major release of that year, the record earned Barbra a second Grammy Award for best female pop vocal performance, and shot to #1 on the *Billboard* charts. Beginning and ending with songs from *Funny Girl*—"Absent Minded Me" (cut from the final score) opens side one, and "People" closes side two—the recording is filled with dramatic ballads by Broadway composers that play to

Streisand's theatrical strengths: Irving Berlin's "Supper Time," Bock and Harnick's "Will He Like Me?", Arlen and Capote's "Don't Like Goodbyes." The vocals are so laden with emotion that Barbra does indeed score as the "actress who sings." And, lest anyone forget it, on the back cover of the album the song listing is bracketed by six headshot photos ranging in image from Lolita-like waif to dramatic diva. Nice photos all, but no one even needed the reminder; great singing like this tells the entire story by itself. Ironically, given the superb ballads contained on the recording, the best cut may in fact be the cheekiest—Cy Coleman and Carolyn Leigh's "When in Rome (I Do as the Romans Do)." Sung with a playful sexuality that's downright erotic, this cut is a textbook lesson in why Barbra hit it so big so quickly: Aside from the great voice, this girl was just plain fun to be around and kept life interesting. It's a sense of fun that dissipated over the years, but sure was great while it lasted.

It was at this juncture in her career that the cross-pollination strategy devised by Barbra and manager Martin Erlichman began in earnest; while starring nightly in *Funny Girl* on Broadway, she also filmed her first—dazzling—television special, which in turn yielded two hit recordings: *My Name Is Barbra* and *My Name Is Barbra, Two.* . . . The former, released concurrently with the airing of the special, contained seven songs from the television special, songs centering on the child/woman dichotomy presented at the beginning of the hour: "My Name Is Barbara" (with the additional a), "A Kid Again/I'm Five" (complete with a lyric change from television to recording, so that on record she can refer to turning five on her actual birthday of April 24; even as a fully exuberant twenty-three-year-old, Barbra knew and insisted that "every little detail plays a part"), and "Where Is the Wonder."

Side two begins with "I Can See It" from *The Fantasticks,* a paean to the excitement that lies just over the horizon (and a song that would resurface as the opening number on the *A Happening in Central*

A BREAK IN THE RECORDING STUDIO. IN CONTROL FROM THE VERY FIRST SESSION. *PHOTOFEST*

Park recording). Barbra was singing this song, whether on record or on the television screen, to all of the outcasts, to all those who needed more out of their lives, and it solidified the very personal connection adoring fans felt to Barbra. Best of all, the album concluded with "Why Did I Choose You" and "My Man." The former song, painting a picture of love through the ages, the latter serving as the quintessential torch song, both showcased Barbra at her larger-than-life, dramatic best. Climbing all the way to #2 on the *Billboard* listings, the album garnered Barbra another Grammy as best female pop vocalist. Most important, this continued pairing with Peter Matz was already resulting in fully realized albums that stood comparison with the Frank Sinatra/Nelson Riddle masterpieces of the 1950s.

Never one to miss a great marketing opportunity, after recording new material, Barbra placed the *My Name Is Barbra* television-special fashion medley on the ensuing new album, called it *My Name Is Barbra, Two. . . .* , added a cover photo from the special, and watched the album hit #2 on the charts. This was not a recycled compilation, as would happen with unfortunate frequency in the later decades of her recording career, but rather fresh material complete with one helluva great medley.

The arranging and conducting chores split evenly between Matz and Sinatra favorite Don Costa, the album opened with the ultra-dramatic "He Touched Me" (from Elliott Gould's short-lived Broadway musical *Drat! The Cat!* wherein he sang it as "She Touched Me"). Beginning quietly with a softly tinkling piano, the song builds to a thunderous climax complete with horns, percussion, and swelling orchestra; when Barbra sings "He touched me, and nothing, nothing is the same," so intense is the vocal that one wonders if the earth fell off its axis after he touched her. *Whew.* It's almost, but not quite, over-wrought, and the song reappeared in her '94 concerts as a fan favorite.

The Gershwins' "I Got Plenty of Nothin'" is heard both in toto and as part of the fashion medley, "The Kind of Man a Woman Needs" covers the romantic love angle, and the fashion medley caps off the recording: Peter Matz pulls out all the stops with a wailing brass section on the medley, and Streisand belts her way through "Give Me the Simple Life" and "Nobody Knows You When You're Down and Out." These vocals are a very long way from the sweet lilt of Doris Day and Jo Stafford, or the whispered insinuations of Peggy Lee, but they are great fun; not only is Streisand in terrific voice, but she is having fun with the lyrics as well. It's a freewheeling, seemingly casual yet fully thought-out performance, and it works beautifully.

Unlike the *My Name Is Barbra* and *My Name Is Barbra, Two . . .* recordings, the *Color Me Barbra* television special soundtrack, released in 1966, consisted solely of material contained in the program itself (and is therefore analyzed in the context of the special itself). *Color Me Barbra* was another extraordinary achievement, but even after this series of unmitigated successes, it was at this point that the naysayers began to quibble about the Streisand vocal style: too loud, they said, too much *geshrey*ing, too many "my man done wronged me" torch songs, too much, too, too, too . . .

After a charming two-song contribution to legendary composer and first champion Harold Arlen's solo LP (a rollicking, campy "Ding Dong! The Witch Is Dead" and the moving "House of Flowers"), Streisand's response to this criticism was to release two of the finest albums of her entire career. Artistically sound—inspired, even—but not big sellers, it took thirty-five years for *Je M'Appelle Barbra* and *Simply Streisand* to attain the status of gold recordings (the certifications were announced on the occasion of her sixtieth birthday). At the time, the relative lack of commercial success for these two releases obscured the fact that they were the two most consistent albums of her career to date.

Je M'Appelle Barbra found all traces of the Brooklyn inflections virtually banished, and for the first time, paired Streisand with Michel Legrand. Legrand's elongated melody lines seemed custom made for the Streisand vocal chords, and the album featured both French and English versions of the song "Le Mur (I've Been Here)"; as the liner notes point out, this song, written for Edith Piaf, who died before she was ever able to perform it, was withheld from French singers by composer Charles Dumont and lyricist Michel Vaucaire once they heard that Streisand was preparing an album of French songs. The album contained "Ma Premiere Chanson," a sweet, somewhat vapid song which served as Streisand's first recorded composition, but soared with better-known compositions. "Autumn Leaves" drips with an understated sense of loss, while "I Wish You Love" represents perhaps the apotheosis of Streisand's "Happy Days Are Here Again"–like signature of inverting the meaning of a song: no sweet nothings for her lover in this version. Rather, this is a bitter, ironic, eleven-o'clock number powerfully showcasing a scorned woman who wishes her lover anything but love.

And—as if anticipating the naysayers who would voice the how-dare-this-Brooklyn-girl-sing-Piaf-songs-in-French line of criticism, Streisand simply recruited Maurice Chevalier to write the liner notes for the album: "She is mad with talent and more gifted than any human being should be permitted to be . . . her artistry is new, impulsive, staggering. We bow to you 'grande petite Madame.'" Indeed. So there.

Her next release, *Simply Streisand,* was just what the title said. No gimmicks. Definitive interpretations of "More Than You Know," "The Nearness of You," and "All the Things You Are." Great singer meets great song; it was all in service of the songs. No embellishments. Unless you count the heartfelt liner notes written by no less than Richard Rodgers as an embellishment. Wrote Rodgers: "No one is talented enough to sing with the depth of a fine cello or the lift of a climbing bird. Nobody that is, except Barbra." In nearly the last of the legend-praises-Barbra liner notes (only Leonard Bernstein was to follow), Rodgers states, "She makes our musical world a much happier place than it was before." On the basis of this CD, she did indeed, and Rodgers himself must have been very pleased with her haunting version of "My Funny Valentine."

How exactly did the liner notes by Rodgers, Styne, Cahn, and Arlen come about? Why did these legendary composers/lyricists so willingly sing Streisand's praises? After all, they were not lavishing such effusive praise on other singers. The answer would appear to be twofold: On an artistic level, the composers recognized her extraordinary singing talent, and clearly felt that her vocals justified such encomiums. On a commercial level, these great composers were also businessmen with publishing interests, and clearly understood that in a musical world increasingly dominated by rock music, Barbra Streisand represented a rare opportunity for their songs to be heard by a large, money-paying and record-buying audience.

As for the *Simply Streisand* album itself, it is, like the best of the Sinatra concept albums, a masterpiece complete unto itself. There is no belting. Beautifully arranged by Ray Ellis, one standard follows another: "My Funny Valentine," "The Boy Next Door," "I'll Know," Nothing gets in the way of her unprecedented attention to the lyrics. More completely than ever before, Streisand phrases the lyrics, letting the near-perfect marriage of music and words speak for itself. It is, arguably, her finest album of all, with the possible exception of *The Broadway Album*. Long after Barbra herself and all of her contemporaries have left the scene, her voice on this recording will still resonate. In her readings of these ten classic American songs, so much genuine feeling is expressed by Barbra and felt by the listener that the full range of emotions is experienced. As happens with all truly great popular art, Streisand here creates a pocket of order and understanding in the midst of life's chaos. The work contained in this recording is really that good.

Great as the album was, it could not hide a disturbing fact: It did not reach the top of the charts, did not attain gold record status, and was perceived by the increasingly important youth market as the work of someone behind the times, of someone who at age twenty-five was in danger of being perceived as a young old fogey. From rebel to establishment icon in seven short years. *Whew.* The unthinkable was mentioned: Was Streisand no longer commercially viable?

The crisis was momentarily averted over the next year by three special releases, the first of which, *A Christmas Album,* ranks amongst the most popular of her career. This collection of seasonal favorites neatly sidestepped the issue of appealing to the youth market because it seemed to be the one time of year that the record-buying youth market deemed it acceptable to listen to old pop standards, not to mention sacred songs. Here, the time-tested popular classics ranged from a rollicking "Jingle Bells" to the poignant Judy Garland film ballad "Have Yourself a Merry Little Christmas." Mixing the secular (arranged and conducted by Marty Paich) on tunes such as "White Christmas," with the holy (arranged and conducted by Ray Ellis) on songs such as "The Lord's Prayer" and Gounod's "Ave Maria," there isn't one weak cut on the entire recording, a recording that continues to sell well thirty-eight years after its initial release. In the liner notes for Barbra's 2001 *Christmas Memories* CD, Barbra's longtime Artist and Repertoire executive Jay Landers wrote that when she recorded *A Christmas Album,* Barbra was getting over a cold, a fact which resulted in a slight huskiness being added to her voice; this very slight throati-ness is barely noticeable and in fact only adds to the genuine emotion she invests in these classics.

The film triumph and concurrent soundtrack release of *Funny Girl* followed next, and in the newest touch of cross-medium exposure, the soundtrack to the television special *A Happening in Central Park* was released to coincide with the 1968 airing of the concert. All of these recordings proved successful, but Columbia Records and Streisand felt the need to shake things up, to craft a younger image for the twenty-seven-year-old singer. And thus began Streisand's first, very tentative, steps towards the rock music which totally dominated the charts: the album entitled *What About Today?*

To listen to *What About Today?* is to hear a Barbra Streisand who is hesitant for the first time in her career. Released in 1969, the album displays an uncertainty that possibly reflected the country's unease. One year after the assassinations of Dr. Martin Luther King, Jr. and Robert Kennedy, protests against the Vietnam war raged, the Black Panthers were at the height of their influence, the Stonewall uprising in New York City showcased the beginnings of the gay pride move-ment, and the terms "feminist" and "male chauvinist" entered every-day parlance. America was a country divided against itself, a state of affairs nowhere better reflected than in the fact that the middle-American "silent majority" had succeeded in propelling Richard Nixon to a razor-thin victory over Hubert Humphrey in the 1968 presidential election.

In an America so divided, it wasn't just that rock music ruled the day. It was the fact that the rock-and-roll world seemingly possessed nothing but scorn for the Tin Pan Alley standards and singing exemplified not only by Frank Sinatra and Dean Martin, but also by Barbra Streisand, a woman the same age as many of these rockers. Determined to change her image, Streisand recorded *What About Today?* Unfortunately, the end result is an album that is neither fish nor fowl. Rather it is an uneasy mixture of Michel Legrand/Alan and Marilyn Bergman traditional pop songs, such as "Ask Yourself Why," and three songs by John Lennon and Paul McCartney: "Goodnight," "With a Little Help from My Friends," and an embarrassing rendition of "Honey Pie." Because Barbra Streisand is uncomfortable singing on the beat—the foundation of rock-and-roll singing—the end result was a Streisand album pleasing to neither the traditionalists nor the rock generation.

Sporting a then-startling Afro-style wig on the cover, Streisand's discomfort mirrored the public's. Who was that on the cover? It is no accident that the liner notes reflected this split world; no rock legend provided Streisand with liner notes. Instead, Streisand herself wrote the dedication, to "Young people who shout down mediocrity."

Any acceptance by the rock world was not helped by her next two releases, the soundtracks for *Hello, Dolly!* and *On a Clear Day You Can See Forever*. Never mind that Streisand sounded joyous singing with the great Louis Armstrong on the *Hello, Dolly!* title track, or that the *Clear Day* title song provided her with a sterling Nelson Riddle arrangement that would become a concert staple for her in the 1990s. Her old-fashioned image persisted, right down to the bouffant hairdos and chiffon gowns.

Being very to the point and blunt used to be a weapon for me. But I'm not as defensive anymore. I just really am blunt. That saves me a lot of time and also loses a lot of friends.
—Barbra Streisand, *LIFE* magazine, January 9, 1970

Nineteen seventy and 1971 saw a change in Streisand's image and singing, with the release of *Stoney End* and *Barbra Joan Streisand*. Gone were the elaborate hairdos and fancy gowns, and similarly banished were the pop standards of the past four decades. In their place, the material Barbra chose with famed rock music producer Richard Perry for *Stoney End* represented a who's who of singer-songwriters circa 1970: Joni Mitchell—"I Don't Know Where I Stand," Laura Nyro— "Hands Off the Man (Film Flam Man)" and "Time and Love," Randy Newman—"Let Me Go" and "I'll Be There." The title track became a top ten hit, and the album even had a bit of a rock feel to it; electric guitars figure far more prominently than on any previous Streisand recording, as do background singers (including Clydie King and Vanetta Fields, later to resurface as the Oreos in *A Star Is Born*.)

It's not bad singing—her vocal gifts make that nearly impossible. Barbra treats the songs with respect—too much respect. It's the vocal equivalent of walking on eggshells, because just as on the *Classical Barbra* album, albeit for very different reasons, she can't totally relax. Barbra Streisand does not feel these songs in her bones, and as a result, the performances remain competent but a little pale. Streisand, a great original artist, ends up sounding like she is imitating Laura Nyro on no fewer than three cuts. The end result is far superior to anything on *What About Today?* but it's also never particularly inspired.

Barbra Joan Streisand followed next, and with long straight hair framing her face, a blue-jeaned and tie-dyed Barbra attempted to rock with the all-female rock group Fanny on Carole King's "Where You Lead." If the results throughout the album weren't particularly convincing, they were also not an embarrassment (with the possible exception of a misreading of John Lennon's "Mother," complete with Barbra singing/belting Lennon's primal scream). The problem lay in the fact that this Richard Perry–produced album juxtaposed the Carole King–penned rock lite songs with Bacharach and David's "One Less Bell to Answer/A House Is Not a Home" and the Legrand/

Bergmans "The Summer Knows"; it only takes one listening to realize that these dramatic ballads are where her musical soul lies. She is so at ease with the drama inherent in these story songs that her singing simply soars, leaving the earnest attempts at rock and roll by the wayside.

By the time of the release of her 1972 *Live Concert at the Forum,* in support of George McGovern's presidential campaign, Streisand seemed to have won grudging acceptance from the college-age men and women with whom she appeared somewhat desperate to connect. The album achieves a much more fluid blend of standards ("My Man," "People," "On a Clear Day") with relaxed interpretations of rock numbers such as "Make Your Own Kind of Music," "Stoney End," and particularly a first-rate and Grammy-nominated "Sweet Inspiration/Where You Lead." Especially in that medley, the horn blowing, tambourine playing and backup singers work well with the shortened, punched-up phrasing that Barbra uses, and for once the attempt at rock singing really works. The pot smoking monologue may seem an overly determined display of hipness, but in the end, it's a fun concert with Barbra in good voice.

By sheer force of will, by dint of her increasing interest in feminist concerns, and perhaps most of all because of her outspoken liberal politics, which had earned her a place on President Nixon's "enemies list," Streisand was back on the popular scene and back on the charts with gold records. All of which makes the irony even more pronounced that the career high-water mark which followed hewed to the most traditional of all paths—a simple, nostalgic ballad whose appeal was summed up in its title, "The Way We Were."

The film *The Way We Were,* released in the fall of 1973, provided an America exhausted from the Vietnam War and reeling from the increasingly serious revelations of President Nixon's involvement with the Watergate coverup, with a romantic bath in the seemingly simpler America of the 1930s, 40s, and 50s. (And the message of the movie, of

course, was that it never was an innocent, carefree past.) The film provided an audience the chance to revel in a classic mismatched love
story: the golden boy (Robert Redford) and the loudmouthed, pushy
(read: ethnic) broad (Streisand), who saw only the best in him and demanded that he not settle for less. Framing the opening credits and
end titles was the ultra-romantic Marvin Hamlisch, Alan and Marilyn
Bergman title tune: Opening with a gentle, seamlessly hummed
melody, Streisand's vocal widens with the words, "Memories light the
corners of my mind," and the words "misty water-colored memories"
are heard, as silent, sun-dappled shots of college life in the 1930s flash
onscreen. By the time Streisand vocally asks the poignant question,
"Can it be that it was all so simple then, or has time rewritten every
line?" the listener is hooked. The melody lingers, the words resonate,
and Barbra Streisand had herself a bona fide smash, complete with a
#1 single and two hit albums: the film's soundtrack and a hastily as-
sembled *The Way We Were* vocal album.

The film rose to #1 at the box office and Streisand garnered that
which she craved most of all: critical approval of her acting, followed
by an Academy Award nomination as Best Actress. Never again in her
career would she find such perfect synergy (although the 1994 concerts came close). She was at the top of the record charts—who cared
if it was old fashioned, it sold! She was queen of the box office, and
praised by public and critics alike for her acting. At this one moment
in 1974, Streisand was indeed "in all of the world so far, the greatest,
greatest, star." In the enviable position of mulling over how and where
to follow up this astonishing success, Streisand's answer came from a
most unexpected source. It proved to be an answer which reverberated
through every aspect of her life and career.

That answer took the form of Jon Peters, celebrity hairdresser to
the stars, who first met Barbra when he designed her wigs for the
lightweight comedy *For Pete's Sake*. Peters, a handsome, streetwise
man who had dropped out of school at age fourteen, was not intimi-

dated by Streisand's celebrity, and upon their first meeting he both complimented Streisand on her appearance and told the chronically late diva not to keep him waiting ever again. Intrigued by this forthright, even abrasive manner, Streisand took the bait, and the duo were soon not only living together, but collaborating professionally as well. Outrage greeted Peters' participation in her recording and film ventures, but it soon became apparent that doing business with America's #1 female movie and recording star meant doing business with Jon Peters. The proudly feminist Streisand seemed to almost enjoy deferring to Peters, and so total was his involvement in her career that for the first time since the early 1960s, Martin Erlichman no longer served as Streisand's personal manager. Taking over all roles, Peters oversaw the years from the mid seventies to 1984, years when Streisand enjoyed her greatest popular success but worked on projects of decidedly lesser artistic merit.

Peters' first involvement with Streisand's career was in co-producing *Butterfly,* an album he felt would showcase the hip, indeed sexual, Streisand he knew. Critical reviews ran the gamut, but decades later on *Larry King Live,* Barbra herself referred to the album as the album she cared for least in her recording career. Such was Streisand's popularity at this point that the album still sold well, and while not the worst of her recordings—it does contain silken readings of "I Won't Last a Day Without You" and "Since I Don't Have You"—it clearly does not merit a particularly high place in the Streisand oeuvre. On the negative side of the ledger are the gospel-flavored "Grandma's Hands," and the reggae-sounding "Guava Jelly," the latter vocal seeming to totally lack any understanding and natural empathy for the material. Perhaps the most charitable assessment would be that Broadway divas do not take naturally to singing "Ooh baby, here I am. Come rub it on my belly like guava jelly."

The soundtrack to *Funny Lady,* the successful film sequel to *Funny Girl,* found Streisand back in familiar show-biz territory, and featured a knock-out rendition of Kander and Ebb's "How Lucky Can You Get." Streisand alone on a darkened Broadway stage, belting out a snappy showtune in a bitter, ironic "Happy Days"–like manner—this showcased the diva at her dramatic, urgent best. The Rupert Holmes–produced *Lazy Afternoon* album followed the *Funny Lady* soundtrack, and the mixture of standards ("Moanin' Low"), pop (Stevie Wonder's "You and I") and disco ("Shake Me, Wake Me"), covered all fan bases without seriously alienating any. In fact, listening to the best cuts, like "Moanin' Low" and Holmes's own composition "Letters That Cross in the Mail," makes one wish that Streisand had worked more often with him. Holmes, who clearly loves both the big band sound and that of a full symphonic orchestra, seems to inherently understand what best showcases the Streisand voice, a point under-scored by his terrific arrangement of "You'll Never Know," the clos-ing cut on *Just for the Record.* . . . His use of strings propels her voice forward to maximum effect, and as a composer, he knows just how to play directly to her dramatic instinct. More's the pity that of the mul-tiple cuts he arranged for *Back to Broadway,* only "Warm All Over" has seen the light of day.

At this point, only someone of Streisand's extraordinary appeal could have successively released her next two albums: *Classical Barbra* and the rock-musical remake of *A Star Is Born. Classical Barbra,* com-plete with admiring liner notes from Leonard Bernstein and perhaps the most beautiful photos of her entire career (courtesy of Francesco Scavullo), is a completely respectful yet slightly anemic rendering of art songs by Handel, Fauré, and Bernstein. Clearly anticipating a criti-cal bashing for singing classical music ("How dare she—the chutz-pah!"), Streisand is too reverential. She is tasteful, understated, and ultimately bloodless.

Which is exactly what *A Star Is Born* was not. Hounded by savage press during the filming of the movie, Streisand was criticized not only for allowing Peters to produce the film, but also for producing the album and film (as executive producer) herself. In the new millennium, when even a semi-name in Hollywood has a production company of her own, it is hard to fully appreciate the overwhelmingly negative press Streisand faced for being a female producer. In one sense, Streisand faced down all of the criticism and then some: Both movie and soundtrack reached #1. Admirable for her trailblazing efforts, not just on behalf of herself, but also on behalf of all women in the film industry, Streisand was earning solid feminist credentials and solidifying her position as an icon and trailblazer. Just one problem existed: The wildly popular soundtrack is simply not very good, and proved completely unconvincing as a look at the world of rock music.

While co-star Kris Kristofferson's very limited vocal range huskily emulates those of many rock singers (e.g., Rod Stewart), Streisand's two to three octave range, rounded vowels, and perfect diction are polar opposites of rock singers such as Janis Joplin. Further compounding the problem, Streisand's idea for presenting new rock music was to utilize pop composer/arranger Rupert Holmes—a talented man, but not a rock musician. The resulting "Queen Bee" number does not sound like rock music in the least, and features a torrent of words, more words than any genuine rock song has ever featured. "Lost Inside of You" features a somewhat flat Streisand composition in tandem with Leon Russell, and the last cut on the album, "With One More Look At You/Watch Closely Now," is a rock echo of the *Funny Girl* ending. Streisand, alone on a darkened stage, starts out tentatively, vocally gaining strength, singing through her pain to the triumphant no-matter-the-heartaches-I'll-make-it-on-my-own-and-move-forward ending beloved by her female and gay male fans. The problem is that Streisand's vocal style is totally at odds with the rock world ethos: Rock musicians, as Jon Pareles put it in the *New York Times,* pretend to share their star power with the arena audience. Streisand, like any true diva, luxuriates in the spotlight for herself, by herself. Look at me.

There are, however, three songs in the film that stand the test of time, none of them bearing any relation to rock and roll. Back on the terra firma of pop music, Streisand and the various composers and lyricists soar. "I Believe in Love" (the Bergmans with Kenny Loggins), the feminist anthem "The Woman in the Moon" (Paul Williams and Kenny Ascher), and especially the Streisand-composed love ballad "Evergreen" (with lyrics by Paul Williams) all resonate by presenting Streisand in pop music concert/recording mode. Echoing "The Way We Were," "Evergreen" begins with tender hummed introductory notes, and as Streisand eases into the lyric, extolling "love soft as an easy chair, love fresh as the morning air," her tone warm and intimate, the listener relaxes along with her. There are no frantic, pumped-up attempts to sound hip. Just a universal sentiment and a voice that astonishes with its purity. The critical reception may have been withering—"Evergreen" excepted—but Streisand's vindcation lay in a #1 single, a #1 album, and two Grammys, one for pop female vocal performance and one for composer of the song of the year. Honored by her peers and the public as a vocalist and composer, Streisand (with Peters) forged on. But—and it began to seem like a major qualifier—did it all represent a case of squandered gifts?

With Peters firmly in control of all aspects of Barbra's professional career, the next four years found Streisand at the height of her commercial success even while she tread water artistically. Such was her popularity that she now regularly topped the album charts and consistently scored hit singles, no mean feat for a Tin Pan Alley traditionalist working in the rock-dominated music world of the late 1970s. *Streisand Superman,* the follow-up album to *A Star Is Born,* found the diva in her most overtly feminist frame of mind. It's a pleasant album, containing the hit single "My Heart Belongs to Me" and several songs written for but unused in *A Star Is Born.* A well-sung version of the Billy Joel classic "New York State of Mind" is probably the album's highlight—a horn-blowing arrangement powered by a driving vocal. The Long Island Piano Man meets the Brooklyn diva on the common

RECORDING AT THE TIME OF *A STAR IS BORN*. PHOTOFEST

ground of New York City. (Billy Joel himself has related the anecdote
that his mother finally considered him a real success when she saw that
Streisand had recorded this New York anthem; never mind the millions of albums Joel himself had already sold—to his mother, Barbra
Streisand meant success.) Ultimately what lingers in memory about
Streisand Superman isn't any of the music, but rather the fourteen photos of Barbra, here a visual dichotomy just as she so often has been a
musical and film contradiction. Still sporting the Afro-style hairdo of
A Star Is Born, clad in a tight-fitting white Superman T-shirt and
shorts, she clenches her fist in a seeming feminist salute, yet at the same
time presents herself with her well-toned butt partially hanging out of
the shorts.

Streisand's next three releases, commercial successes all, wash over
the listener leaving no distinct impression. First up was *Songbird,* one
of the truly forgettable recordings of her career, notable for only one
cut: a lovely, understated double-tracked recording of "Tomorrow"

from the Broadway show *Annie*. Ironically, while thousands of little girls across America belted out leather-lunged versions of this relentlessly upbeat ballad (thousands of little girls who clearly had listened to "Don't Rain on My Parade" many times), Streisand herself underplays the vocal, bringing out a wistful quality in the lyric that vanishes in the hands and lungs of legions of little Ethel Mermans. Funny girl indeed.

Songbird was followed by a second volume of greatest hits which reached #1 on the charts. Such was Streisand's popularity that even the soundtrack for *The Main Event,* comprised of filler music and only one vocal, that of the disco-infused hit single title track, scored heavy sales. Another disco single, a duet with chart-topping Donna Summer entitled "No More Tears (Enough Is Enough)," fueled the sales of Streisand's 1979 concept album entitled *Wet.* The concept behind the album was that each cut contained water, or a reference thereto, in the title. Get it? *Ugh.* The actual song selection followed the pattern begun with *A Star Is Born:* at least one cut co-written by Streisand herself, multiple songs written by the Bergmans, and a pop-oriented hit single to drive the album. At this stage, Streisand's voice remained as beautiful as ever, with every detail of the recording painstakingly tended to, but to what end? Hearts made glad at the thought of hearing the Arlen/Mercer standard "Come Rain or Come Shine" sank when confronted with an arrangement which favored electric guitars over Streisand's vocal (much better is the straightforward full-out vocal version on the "special one song" addendum to the *Timeless* concert CD). The silly Bobby Darin novelty number "Splish Splash" degenerates into mindless giggling and has no conceivable reason for inclusion other than being shoehorned in to fit the water concept. Just as with the inclusion of "Tomorrow" on *Songbird,* one lovely forgotten ballad serves as a potent reminder of why Streisand remained the greatest theatrical singer of her generation. "Niagara," by Marvin Hamlisch, Carol Bayer Sager, and Bruce Roberts, speaks of lost love and of promises unkept ("But in Niagara, you promised me the moon"), all set against a background of swelling strings. That voice so loved by the microphone once again effortlessly re-establishes an intimate connection with the Mr. and Ms. Lonelyhearts of the world. Yes, she was a movie star living a secluded, literally above-it-all life in Malibu, but when singing a song like "Niagara" she was still *their* Barbra.

With the release of her next album, *Guilty*, Streisand achieved the greatest commercial success of her recording career and became, temporarily at least, America's Barbra. Pairing with the extraordinarily popular Barry Gibb of Bee Gees fame (Barbra proving nothing if not canny in her choice of duet partners), Streisand sounded more relaxed than she had in years. It may have been the chance to sing modern pop songs without even having to attempt rock singing, but the fun she claimed to have had in making the album showed in the end product. No less than three top ten singles resulted from the collaboration: "Woman in Love," "Guilty," and "What Kind of Fool" (the latter a Grammy winner). The lyrics are oftentimes vague to the point of being totally opaque, but Gibbs' melodies are so catchy, so filled with hooks, that they linger in the mind after even one hearing: Many a listener tried unsuccessfully to forget the beat of the title track:

> *And we have nothing to be guilty of*
> *Our love*
> *Can climb any mountain.*

Streisand's forceful tones seem to invest the lyrics with more meaning than they really have, and the lighter-than-air melodies make it impossible for her to overwhelm the material. Even the white-on-white album art seemed to mesh with the airy, sun-drenched feel of the album. The songs may not be classic, but the resulting product (and it was a product—a meeting of two pop titans on a newly discovered middle ground) proved to be totally pleasurable, if slightly disposable, popular music. Not only did it become Streisand's best-selling album ever, but it also proved to be far and away her most successful attempt at contemporary pop—if not rock—singing.

Memories, basically yet another greatest hits collection (released only three albums after the previous greatest hits collection) and fleshed out with a handful of new songs including the ubiquitous "Memory" from Andrew Lloyd Webber's *Cats,* followed *Guilty.* Successful without breaking any new territory, *Memories* functioned simply as a way to fulfill a contractual obligation to Columbia Records for that year's album release. The true follow-up to *Guilty* lay in a genuine roll of the dice on Streisand's part; just as *The Way We Were* was followed up by the contentious *A Star Is Born,* so too did Streisand once again gamble her power, success, and career on another controversial, high-profile, big-stakes production: *Yentl.*

Released in 1983, *Yentl* represented a nearly extinct species: the original screen musical. Ever since the groundbreaking 1972 Bob Fosse film of *Cabaret,* which placed all of the musical numbers in the context of the actual Kit Kat Klub cabaret, audiences demanded a reason or realistic (preferably theatrical) setting for characters to break into song. Without that reason, contemporary audiences would quite literally tune out.

Working with favorite composer/lyricists Michel Legrand/Alan and Marilyn Bergman, Streisand solved this dilmemna through eleven musical numbers which represented Yentl's interior thoughts. Since Yentl lived the repressed life of a girl masquerading as a boy in order to study, her private thoughts could only be expressed in musical soliloquys. When the pressure of such a closeted, frustrating life became too much to bear, Yentl's inner passions burst forth in these interior musical interludes. The resulting music and lyrics proved to be a cohesive, deeply felt score that represented the most sustained achievement of the Bergmans' and Legrand's careers, and contained some of Streisand's most passionately involved singing.

Upon initial release, the virtues of the score were obscured by the sustained controversy which greeted Streisand's attempt to be the first woman ever to write, star in, produce, and direct a major Hollywood film. The familiar refrain of "how dare she" led to charges of megalomania, which led to the considerable assets of the score being overlooked. Legrand's flowing, sustained musical lines (or as Streisand herself termed them, his "swooping melodies") were neatly matched by the Bergmans' succession of lyrical questions: "Where Is It Written?"; "Papa, Can You Hear Me?" The lyrical questions asked by Yentl actually reinforced the public's knowledge of Streisand's continuing fight against industry barriers: Why couldn't she produce? Why couldn't she direct? Where was it written indeed. As with any true icon, Streisand's professional work, private life, and the public perception thereof all reinforced each other, heightening the debate. Musically speaking, just as happened on the *Je M'appelle Barbra* album, Streisand reveled in the billowing, nearly swooning melodies penned by Legrand. Her seamless legato not only intact after twenty years of recording, but indeed burnished by the warmer tone that had developed with age, she invested the score with the passion so lacking in efforts such as *Wet* and *Songbird*. It is as if Streisand is declaring, "There is a reason for this recording. These songs are for my father. Pay attention." In point of fact, when deciding whether to make *Yentl,* Streisand visited a psychic along with her brother Sheldon. She has related that the psychic received two messages from "Daddy." The first message was "Sorry," and the second was "Sing proud." Commented Streisand: "I made *Yentl* and I did sing proud."

There may be a bland sameness to some of the score (three versions of "No Wonder" seems excessive, and "Tomorrow Night" runs an unnecessarily long time) but Legrand's and the Bergmans' knowledge of Streisand resulted in a score that played to her strengths. The score and film culminate in an all-stops-out vocal on "A Piece of Sky." The listener knows that the song represents a Streisand archetype, but the damn thing still works like hell: a tentative beginning followed by a marshalling of resources, the voice gathering strength and urgency as it rides the crest of a huge symphony orchestra, climaxing in a bell-like final note held for an eternity—a triumphant declaration of will. A clear echo of her first act closing "Parade" showstoppers, "Don't Rain on My Parade" and "Before the Parade Passes By," the *Yentl* score, as exemplified by "A Piece of Sky," ends on a personal synergistic note: Broadway belter meets triumphant film director/diva, meets movie which mirrors Barbra's own life, meets personality and public icon. At the time of initial release, it was impossible to fully separate out the different strands of Streisand's obsession with *Yentl,* a fact which hid the strengths of the recording. It was certainly no accident that Streisand's 1994 concert tour climaxed in a live duet with her celluloid Yentl character, just as her "final" concerts in 2000 utilized the Yentl score as—what else—the Act I showstopping closer. By this time the public had grown increasingly familiar with the score; indeed the phrase "Papa, can you hear me?" had entered the public consciousness—more specifically the gay public consciousness—strongly enough to function as a gag line on *Will & Grace,* the groundbreaking gay sitcom.

Given the virtues of the *Yentl* score, it was all the more curious that Streisand's next album, *Emotion,* represented what may well be the nadir of her recording career. It is not that the singing is bad—it is not subpar in any manner of speaking—but Streisand takes a huge step backwards in a recording which represents yet another touch-all-of-the-bases pop recording. *Emotion* represents a collection of songs which could have been recorded by *any* artist, the first and only time that could be said about a Streisand album. No reason on earth exists for Barbra Streisand to have recorded any of these songs. The album simply followed the by now familiar pattern of a duet here ("Make No Mistake, He's Mine" with Kim Carnes) and a Streisand-penned song there ("You're a Step in the Right Direction," written with John

Mellencamp), with the album fleshed out by songs from established rock composers ("Left in the Dark" by Jim Steinman). Yet in the end, even the title song reunion with *Stoney End* producer Richard Perry, is forgettable, and the only song which registers at all is Streisand's own composition of "Here We Are At Last" (one of the musical themes Streisand composed for her film *Nuts*, with lyrics by then-boyfriend Richard Baskin). Positioned as the closing track to the *Emotion* album, "Here We Are At Last" is a sweetly lyrical traditional melody, which seemed to point the way to what would be a full musical recovery and the single greatest recording of her career: *The Broadway Album*.

Streisand had mulled over the idea of an album of theater songs for years, the idea originally occurring to her when recording "There Won't Be Trumpets" (Sondheim) and "A Quiet Thing" (Kander and Ebb) for *Butterfly*. (The songs were cut from the release of *Butterfly* and reappeared only on the four-disc boxed set *Just For the Record*. . . .) Streisand has claimed that Columbia Records fought the idea of the seemingly noncommercial, middle-of-the-road *Broadway Album*. However, given her own determined pursuit of commercial success, and her sometimes desperate attempts to craft a younger image, it would more likely have been a reluctance on both parts until 1983. Perhaps it was the realization that the *Emotion* LP contained anything *but* emotion—an essentially meaningless disc. Whatever the reason, Streisand plunged headlong into a return to her roots—American musical theater. With her trademark obsessive pursuit of perfection, she teamed up with the two men who became the key to the project's artistic success: arranger Peter Matz and composer/lyricist Stephen Sondheim.

The reunion with Matz ensured that the arrangements were in the hands of the man who worked with Streisand on her earliest, most intensely theatrical recordings, an arranger who intuitively understood how best to frame her grandiloquent dramatic readings. Finding herself drawn to the full range of the Sondheim canon—from *West Side Story* (1957) to *Sunday in the Park with George* (1984)—Streisand began a one-on-one working relationship with the man universally regarded as the greatest composer/lyricist in the musical theater today. Most important, the musically adventurous, lyrically dense Sondheim songs proved to be so complex in and of themselves that Streisand could not overwhelm the songs, as so often happened when she attacked lesser pop confections. Instead, singing live with a full studio orchestra, she relaxed—indeed soared—releasing an album filled with extraordinarily moving versions of theatrical gems that really did constitute the three-act plays Jule Styne had so long ago stated she made out of songs. (In some ways her own harshest critic, Streisand, while working on *The Broadway Album,* went back and listened to her first two albums, and in her own words ". . . just cringed listening to some of the performances. Although I had a purer reedlike sound in those days, I think my singing then was often overly dramatic and screechy.")

Working intensely with Sondheim, Streisand invested the songs with a pure emotional directness which had been missing from her coldly perfect studio pop recordings for years. She opened the album with Sondheim's revised and custom-tailored lyrics for "Putting It Together," lyrics which resonated with references to her publicized artistic struggles: "Even when you get some recognition/Everything you do you still audition." There were bona fide artistic reasons for recording every single song included on the album, with Streisand ranging from the tender ("Can't Help Lovin' That Man") through the yearning ("If I Loved You") to the classic ("I Loves You Porgy").

It is with the Sondheim selections, however, that Streisand truly dazzled vocally and dramatically. Just as Streisand has always considered herself an actress who sings, Sondheim is a dramatist whose form of expression is the popular song. Given the chance to play fully realized three-dimensional characters, Streisand tears into the bitter, acerbic "Ladies Who Lunch" and the propulsive surging anthem to love and commitment, "Being Alive." Asking Sondheim to write additional lyrics for the second bridge in his most famous song, "Send In the Clowns," Streisand beautifully underplays the rueful self-awareness of the lyric, matching the mournful melody every step of the way. In an album of continuous highlights, the only mis-step is the ill-conceived David Foster electronic setting for "Somewhere," a mistake rectified in the intensely theatrical, just-over-the-horizon renditions of the song with which she concluded her 1994 and 2000 concerts. In what was almost an embarrassment of riches, there were additional hints of what could have been: Sondheim and Streisand worked on songs from *Gypsy,* combining that driving anthem to ambition, "Some People," with "Rose's Turn," a full-fledged nervous breakdown in song. If that inspired combination didn't make the final cut, it almost didn't matter. For once the liner notes paying homage to Streisand were right on the money. In the words of the Bergmans: "Here the singer and the song are worthy of each other. They are the best." The critics cheered, the album hit #1, and a female pop vocal Grammy Award resulted. In a recording career of many peaks, *The Broadway Album* represented the highest.

Streisand couldn't really top *The Broadway Album* with another studio recording, and smartly opted instead to next release the 1986 live recording of her *One Voice* concert. This one-night Democratic Party fundraiser, held in a specially constructed ampitheater on Streisand's Malibu estate grounds, found her in good voice, and while little of the material was new, there was a sweetly sung version of "Over the Rainbow" dedicated to Judy Garland—one diva saluting another. Never one to miss an opportunity for cross-media exposure, the concert was filmed for subsequent broadcast on HBO; if the public could not yet see Streisand in concert, this invitation-only concert offered the public a tantalizing glimpse of what they had been missing. True to form, the broadcast provided the video equivalent of admiring liner notes in the form of fulsome tributes from Bette Midler, Henry Winkler, and Whitney Houston.

Nineteen eighty-seven came and went with only the release of music composed by Streisand for the film *Nuts;* Joked Barbra: "For some time I had dreamed of scoring a movie. When I produced *Nuts* the dream became a reality—after all, who else would hire me . . . or fire me?!" It was thus not until 1988 that Streisand released her first studio album in three years, *Till I Loved You.*

The problem with *Till I Loved You* is not that it is bad—it isn't—but that it represents a step backwards from the challenging material of *The Broadway Album.* A concept album loosely fitted around "Girl meets boy, girl loves boy, girl loses boy, girl and boy might get together again," the album features songs by Burt Bacharach and Carole Bayer Sager, and of course multiple songs by the Bergmans. It's not a bad idea for an album. Streisand after all is the ultimate female romantic—but her pipes overwhelm the songs. Because she invests such urgency in her vocal interpretations, Streisand needs material that won't collapse under the weight of her yearning, ultra-dramatic approach. The title track, a duet with then-boyfriend Don Johnson, is a pleasant Maury Yeston song undercut by Johnson's thin voice. The surging melody line of the one theater song included, Andrew Lloyd Webber's "All I Ask of You" *(Phantom of the Opera),* works better, but the Legrand/Bergman "On My Way to You" is inferior to their work on *Yentl.* The concluding song, "One More Time Around," leaves the same impression that the entire album does—it's just a case of marking time. The exhilarating freedom of *The Broadway Album,* the sense of joy Streisand felt singing with that full live orchestra, is here replaced by a rather cold electronic professionalism. Yes, there is meticulous craftsmanship, layer upon layer from start to finish, but the finished product is a work of the brain, not of the heart.

What proved more disturbing was the recurrent thought that

Streisand was simply not challenging herself as great artists should. With all those extravagant gifts at her disposal, one felt she should be investigating the catalogue of the great American songbook, recording albums devoted to the very best composers and lyricists: Gershwin, Porter, Berlin, Kern, Schwartz, Dorothy Fields, and Johnny Mercer. Ella Fitzgerald's brilliant recording career is centered around her great songbook tributes to these extraordinary pop composers. Sinatra's concept albums with Nelson Riddle, and even his straightforward pop recordings such as "Ring A Ding Ding," were filled with the work of the masters. Beginning at age fifty, Rosemary Clooney built an entirely new twenty-five-year recording career on the Concord label exploring those golden-age composers. Streisand, the last of the great romantics, clearly felt those brilliant composers in her very soul. Her best recordings, especially from the early stages of her career, were full of original, oftentimes brilliant interpretations of their work. And what was her legacy now? "On My Way to You"? "One More Time Around"? Legacy seemed an odd word to apply to the work of a then forty-five-year-old singer, but so vast was her recorded output already, so great her gifts, that the question seemed appropriate. At this stage, no one, least of all Streisand herself, seemed certain of what that legacy was or should be.

Perhaps it was thus no accident that yet another greatest-hits offering followed, this one entitled *A Collection: Greatest Hits . . . and More.* With just a few new songs included, even die-hard Streisand fans were beginning to mutter that it wouldn't kill her to record some new material (at that time, no fewer than nine Streisand releases contained a recording of "People"). And while the 1991 release of *The Prince of Tides* soundtrack didn't stop such grumbling, the soundtrack did feature a wonderfully moody score by James Newton Howard that perfectly fit the haunted characters of the film. The CD also included two Streisand vocals not in the film (after all, who would believe a singing psychiatrist?!). The two songs were "Places That Belong to

You"—the musical theme from the film outfitted with a new lyric by—who else—the Bergmans. The second song was a gorgeously sung version of the standard "For All We Know" (Coots/Lewis): In a performance as good as any she has delivered, Streisand luxuriates in a beautifully crafted Johnny Mandel orchestration and delivers on every one of the lyric's romantic images: "We won't say goodnight until the last minute . . . For all we know, this may only be a dream." What makes the performance even more extraordinary is that before record-ing this song, Streisand had not sung in two years—no studio sessions, no concerts, no nothing. To think that a two-year silence could be broken by such a beautiful recording is staggering, and adds to the sense of frustration all Streisand observers have felt at one time or an-other. (Also of interest is the fact that concurrent with the release of *Prince of Tides,* Bette Midler starred in and produced her own long-gestating pet project, the nostalgic drama with music *For the Boys,* a film which included her own version of "For All We Know." To com-pare the two versions is to hear the difference between a very talented singer—Midler—and a truly great theatrical singer—Streisand. One can only imagine the reaction of each diva when they found out that the other was also releasing "For All We Know" . . .)

Nineteen ninety-one also saw the release of the four-disc retrospec-tive entitled *Just for the Record. . . .* While parts of the release had a greatest-hits feel to them, over half of the material had never before been released: Two discs represented material from the 1960s, with a third disc featuring material culled from the 70s, and a final disc center-ing on the 80s. What makes the boxed set fascinating is not just the evo-lution of the career and material, but the evolution of Streisand's voice.

Beginning with a 1955 acetate recording of "You'll Never Know" by the then thirteen-year-old Barbra (the 1991 recording of the same song by the mature Streisand closes the collection), it is fascinating to follow the dramatic instincts which were already in place during her adolescence. The vibrato used to accentuate emotion, the letter-perfect diction, the edge of hysteria at moments of dramatic urgency—it is clear from the beginning why outsiders of all stripes and romantics of all ages responded to the Streisand voice. "I want— I need—why can't I—you can't stop me—will I ever have" . . . These are the primal emotions the career retrospective makes clear the Streisand voice always and ineffably was able to convey.

The material from the 1960s serves as a potent reminder that Streisand's dignified, remote, imperious presence of the present day is miles away from the kooky, brash singer of "Who's Afraid of the Big Bad Wolf." That nineteen-year-old newcomer wasn't afraid of one damn thing, and relished saying "I'm so far out I'm in." Those were not words proudly spoken by entertainment figures in the still buttoned-down early 1960s, but Streisand reveled in her rebelliousness. These 1960s discs represent a collection of her best-known and most fondly received album cuts, along with special material. The historic duet with Judy Garland is recorded in its entirety, as is the witty Friars Club tribute to Streisand by seven legendary composers: Rodgers, Styne, Coleman, Rome, Herman, Arlen, and Lane. Talk about liner notes coming to life . . . The 60s discs conclude with downright brilliant live performances of "When You Gotta Go" and "In the Wee Small Hours of the Morning" (arranged and conducted by Peter Matz). There's no other word for singing that good. Yes, the lyrics are phrased precisely and tell the story wonderfully, but it is the sheer physical beauty of the voice which awes. And leads one to ask: Why the hell didn't she continue to sing material this strong?

The 70s and 80s discs present a treasure trove of never-released recordings. For starters, there is the smashing rendition of Cole Porter's "You're the Top" sung over the opening and closing credits of *What's Up, Doc?* It is a glorious, freewheeling performance (with a terrific arrangement by Artie Butler) wherein Streisand, singing with co-star Ryan O'Neal, pokes great fun at herself—something that ceased altogether beginning in the 1980s:

O'Neal (singing): "You're the nose . . ."
Streisand: "Watch it."
O'Neal: "I mean on the great Durante."
Streisand: "That's better!"

Interestingly, this cut also emphasizes another aspect of the Streisand appeal: the inherent contrast and tension between her rapid-fire Brooklyn-inflected diction, especially in her earliest film and television appearances, and the warm rounded tones of her singing.

Of special interest are two songs from an unreleased concept album entitled *Between Yesterday and Tomorrow,* an album which was to follow the course of one woman's life. In particular, a beautiful Legrand/Bergmans song entitled "Can You Tell the Moment?" stands out, ending with a quiet musical question as Streisand seamlessly elongates the final words:

> *Maybe in an April shower*
> *Something tells a bud to flower*
> *What is it that tells you*
> *You're a child no more?*

There is an alternative version of "The Way We Were" (which Streisand wittily refers to as "The Way We Weren't"), an audition tape to convince the studios of the viability of *Yentl* ("Everything you do you still audition" indeed), the Broadway ballad "Warm All Over"—it is all fascinating Streisand trivia that showcases the evolution of the voice and style. A few top notes may have been lost over the three decades, the abandoned flinging-about of her talent definitely muted, but in their place has come a mature perspective on life and a greater understanding of the lyrics (e.g., the Sondheim songs). Throughout all four discs stands one all-important constant: a voice that touches the audience and allows Streisand, like Frank Sinatra, to sing of her life and emotions in a manner which mysteriously connects with theirs.

The 1993 release of *Back to Broadway* represented the follow-up to *The Broadway Album* for which fans had been waiting eight years. Entering the charts at #1, the fourth consecutive decade Streisand had achieved a #1 recording, it is a good CD which suffers only in comparison to its more consistent predecessor.

Opening with a sweetly sung version of "Some Enchanted Evening," Streisand surprises by eschewing the traditional stentorian approach to this song in favor of an understated hopefulness, ending on a quiet elongated spinning-out of the final message: "Never let him go." Not surprisingly, the highlights are nearly all Sondheim: a defiant "Everybody Says Don't," a wise, moving version of "Children Will Listen," which fully explores the double-edged meaning of the title, and the romantic yearning of "I Have a Love/One Hand, One Heart," sung with her compatriot in adolescent fervor, Johnny Mathis. Two Andrew Lloyd Webber songs from *Sunset Boulevard,* "With One Look" and especially "As If We Never Said Goodbye," score with their sheer dramatic force: Over-the-top dramatics are entirely appropriate when channeling faded movie star Norma Desmond. A beautiful, wistful version of "I've Never Been In Love Before" from *Guys and Dolls* completes the album's highlights.

It's a minor problem, but a problem nonetheless, that unlike *The Broadway Album, Back to Broadway* contains several missteps. Chief among the mistakes is an unnecessary duet with Michael Crawford on "Music of the Night" from *Phantom of the Opera,* a song which is not particularly effective when sung from the female point of view. There is also a grating electronic "Luck Be a Lady" from *Guys and Dolls,* and one of Streisand's very few mis-cues of a Broadway song: the Gershwins' "The Man I Love." The vocal starts out with the tenderness inherent in the material, but mid-song Streisand's pride in her musical improvisation leads her to actually lose sight of the clean, elegant melody line, thereby undercutting the lyric as well. At this stage of her career, it appears, no one would dare tell her that the vocal could have been better by being simpler.

The CD ends with the powerful "Move On" from Sondheim's *Sunday in the Park with George*. Streisand chooses to frame the song as a meditation on personal relationships; it could just as easily serve as a metaphor for her extraordinary career:

> *I chose and my world was shaken—so what?*
> *The choice may have been mistaken*
> *The choosing was not*
> *Just keep moving on.*

It is a lovely performance of a first-rate song, but in the end, the difference between *Back to Broadway* and the predecessor with which it is inextricably intertwined is summed up in the fact that *The Broadway Album* won Streisand a pop vocal Grammy, while *Back to Broadway* "only" won her a Grammy nomination.

After *Back to Broadway,* it was, unfortunately, back to filler material—to wit, the soundtrack from the Streisand-directed film, *The Mirror Has Two Faces*. This CD contains the musical score for the film composed by Marvin Hamlisch, as well as two Streisand vocals. The first, "All of My Life," was not used in the film, and is a pop ditty which essentially states the same themes found in the song which was used over the closing credits: "I Finally Found Someone," written by Streisand, Hamlisch, J. R. Lange, and Barbra's duet partner Bryan Adams. "I Finally Found Someone," is a pleasant, somewhat forgettable pop song, the entire meaning of which is stated in the title. The song is noteworthy for only two reasons: 1, It gained Streisand a second Academy Award nomination as composer of the best song (losing to Andrew Lloyd Webber and Tim Rice's "You Must Love Me" from *Evita*—a film role she had reportedly rejected years before with the statement, "I refuse to play a fascist"). 2, It provided Streisand with her last top-ten single to date.

The 1997 release of the religious/inspirational CD entitled *Higher Ground* ushered in a new phase in Streisand recordings: CDs containing ideas in synch with what the public wanted to hear her sing, but unfortunately marred by mediocre song selection. *Higher Ground* was inspired by, and dedicated to, the memory of Virginia Clinton Kelley, President Clinton's mother; it was at Mrs. Kelley's funeral that Streisand heard the song "On Holy Ground" and conceived of the album. In fact, the choice of "On Holy Ground" was an inspired one, and the song is far and away the highlight of the CD. It features a driving, powerful performance wherein Streisand, backed by a gospel-sounding choir, builds chorus by chorus to the impassioned vocal conclusion: "We are on holy ground." A trademark bell-clear final note held against a swelling orchestra speaks of total commitment and total belief, which is, of course, the point of the CD. Would that the rest of the CD were as impassioned.

Instead, Streisand meanders—something she has almost never done. She has made mistakes, yes, but these were usually mistakes of commitment. There are overly reverential treatments of "I Believe/ You'll Never Walk Alone," second-tier pop songs such as the "Tell Him" duet with Celine Dion, and a surprisingly unmoving medley of "The Water Is Wide/Deep River." In the end, "On Holy Ground" serves as a one-shot reminder of how powerful a singer Streisand can be, much like "For All We Know" does on *The Prince of Tides* soundtrack. The idea of inspirational songs coming from a voice like Streisand's, a voice that touches the innermost emotions and passions of the public, is a great one, and Streisand's deeply held religious faith makes the closing track of "Avinu Malkeinu" quite moving. Indeed, the CD did manage to touch enough of a chord with the public to sell several million copies; the pity is that the CD could have been much better with less reverence and more of the raw testifying emotion contained in "On Holy Ground."

The exact same problem of a first-class idea combined with second-class material similarly mars the 1999 CD *A Love Like Ours.* After so many years spent singing of lost loves, years of yearning for the one true love first sung about thirty-eight years earlier in "A Sleepin' Bee," she had found her own Prince Charming, handsome Hollywood actor James Brolin. Barbra had fulfilled her deepest dreams, and the public anticipated the release of a CD full not of yearning, but of commitment and happiness. Streisand, the newly married great pop romantic, singing of personal fulfillment—this was a match made in pop-music heaven for the legions of fans who identified with her quest. The problem was simply that the song selection on *A Love Like Ours,* with only three exceptions, was downright uninspired.

The booklet accompanying the CD is filled with numerous shots of Streisand and Brolin: wedding-day photos, pictures on the beach, the happy couple frolicking at sunset. The photos may tell the story of personal happiness, but the songs themselves don't tell much of any story, blending one into another like so much verbal mush. "I've Dreamed of You" becomes "Love Like Ours" becomes "We Must Be Loving Right" becomes "It Must Be You," until there is virtually no vocal definition to separate the endless flow of words. No vocal definition, that is, except on three songs.

The first of these songs, the Gershwins' beautiful "Isn't It a Pity" (a song Streisand and Brolin danced to at their wedding) receives a lovely pure reading from Streisand and fits beautifully with the theme of finding love at a later stage in life. The second top-drawer song is a new pop tune by Melissa Manchester and Tom Snow entitled "Just One Lifetime," and features a performance filled with the sense of urgency and dramatic force of will which separates Streisand from her many imitators. The final great song is the CD-closing remake of "The Music That Makes Me Dance" from the Broadway version of *Funny Girl*. It's a gem of a song, a near perfect blend of words and music, here reworked to contain echoes of "People" and let the world know that Streisand, the queen of make-believe romanticism, has found "The Music That Makes Her Dance" in real life. The canny orchestration conjures the very images of the lovebirds at sunset featured in the CD photos. Barbra's happy and her fans are happy for her, but there's a lot of filler to wade through before that happy ending is reached on the CD. As happens so often with Streisand, she dazzles and frustrates at the same time. Oy.

Streisand's 2001 CD *Christmas Memories* (her second Christmas album) proved to be the most consistently successful CD she had recorded since *The Broadway Album* sixteen years earlier. Released shortly after the terrorist attack of 9/11, the CD seemed to fit neatly with the national mood of gathering loved ones close by. Unlike so many of her most recent CDs, here the song choices are uniformly excellent. Schubert's "Ave Maria" fits nicely as a companion piece to Gounod's "Ave Maria," which she sang on the 1967 *A Christmas Album*. Sondheim revisits an early composition entitled "I Remember," adding a new verse to make it a remembrance of Christmases past, and a first-class Johnny Mandel/Bergmans song entitled "A Christmas Love Song" is an embrace of the holidays filled with honest sentiment. In an album without any second-rate material, there are three standouts: "One God," "I'll Be Home for Christmas," and "What Are You Doing New Year's Eve."

"One God," by Ervin Drake and Jimmy Shirl, features a full-bodied arrangement by Eddie Karem which contains all of the passion and life force so lacking on most of *Higher Ground*. "I'll Be Home for Christmas" is sung with tenderness and a purity of tone which underlines the truth hidden beneath the occasionally hyperbolic liner notes by loyal A & R man Jay Landers; here Streisand really is singing with greater "richness, clarity, and golden tone." Above all, there is an extraordinary rendition of "What Are You Doing New Year's Eve," which brings out all of the hopefulness inherent in the title question, without sacrificing any of Frank Loesser's melodic richness. Listening to Streisand bend notes with ease, gracefully sliding up the scale on the word *eve,* is the fulfillment of Jule Styne's early liner notes writ large; Streisand here give us a three-act play, complete with conflict, rising action, and successful resolution. In other words, given a great American standard, Streisand soars. Given the melodically mushy material, complete with Hallmarklike lyrics, present on so many of the later CDs, she overwhelms the material, thereby serving neither the writers, the public, nor herself.

After such an artistic and commercially satisfying effort (Grammy nomination and platinum sales), hopes were high for the next releases, but Streisand seemed content to offer not just one, but two more CDs which functioned basically as yet further greatest hits collections. *The Essential Barbra Streisand* consisted of a chronological assemblage of hits, beginning with "A Sleepin' Bee" and continuing through "I've Dreamed of You" from *A Love Like Ours.* At this point, even the most die-hard Streisand fan could be forgiven for expressing frustration at yet another release of "People" and "The Way We Were." In a rather cynical move on Streisand's part, the hook for her fans to buy the CD was the inclusion of a paltry two new songs. But for the die-hard fan, the problem with overlooking the release was that both new cuts were extraordinary, as powerful as any Streisand had released. The first is a revisiting of the *Snow White* classic "Someday My Prince Will Come." Originally recorded New Year's Eve 1993, in a terrific arrangement by William Ross that frames an amazingly pure vocal from a then fifty-one-year-old woman, the second version features a symphony orchestra that sounds like a one-hundred-piece ensemble. As with all great artists, there is a point in Streisand's revisiting of the song; if in 1993 she sang wistfully of the prince that the odd-looking heroine

IN THE WAKE OF 9/11, BARBRA'S STIRRING
VERSION OF "YOU'LL NEVER WALK ALONE."
EMMY AWARDS, NOVEMBER 4, 2001. *CORBIS*

still sought, by 2002 the meaning proved different. Streisand had found her prince in James Brolin, and if she still on occasion sounded like a Snow White who could and would demand that Prince Charming show up—and NOW—this last of the great traditional pop vocalists invested every ounce of her passion in the vocal. At last she had provided the happily-ever-after ending which she had not only so long sought for herself, but which also provided hope for her fans, hope that their dreams could come true as well.

The second new cut that soars is another classic revisited: Rodgers and Hammerstein's "You'll Never Walk Alone." First heard in a meandering, lugubriously understated version on *Higher Ground,* this new William Ross arrangement, sung on the Emmy Awards shortly after 9/11, fit the country's then near desperate need for faith and belief after the terrorist attack. Backed by a gospel-inflected choir, Streisand applies her will of iron to a song often unfairly dismissed as suitable only for junior-high assemblies, and turns it into a stirring affirmation of love and togetherness—an affirmation for a country shaken to its foundations. This is real passion, and among the most stirring performances of her career.

Streisand's second 2002 release, *Duets,* was, incredibly enough, another compilation, this one centered around the title concept. Just as on *The Essential Barbra Streisand,* there are a paltry two new songs to hook the buyer, the new songs being forgettable duets with Barry Manilow and Josh Groban. The rest of the material ranges from the sublime ("Get Happy/Happy Days are Here Again" with Judy Garland) to the ridiculous ("Make No Mistake, He's Mine" with Kim Carnes.) Even more than the two Barry Gibbs duets included from *Guilty,* the standout cut on the *Duets* CD is Barbra's duet with herself on "One Less Bell To Answer/A House Is Not a Home." In dealing with the symphonic pop of Burt Bacharach and Hal David, Streisand found the only duet partner capable of matching her crooning urgency—indeed recklessness—on the subject of lost love: herself. Listen to her voice breaking on the word *darling* as she sings, "So Darling, have a heart. Don't let one mistake keep us apart." The listener knows the inflection has been minutely calculated, but damn if it doesn't still work. This woman sings of heartbreak, of emotional extravagance, from the very core of her being. I want. I need. Indeed.

Film

This reputation about being difficult comes from untalented people misunderstanding truly talented ones. Because she's so talented she had a tendency—maybe she still does—to show off a bit. She was always shoving shovelsful of her talent in your face. Jerry Robbins summed her up. He said she does everything wrong but it comes out right.

—Jule Styne, Composer, *Funny Girl*

Barbra Joan Streisand of Brooklyn, New York, hit the movie screens in September 1968 with a dazzling one-woman tour de force in *Funny Girl* which left critics and audiences alike delighted, a public reaction to which the diva herself seemed to say, "Well, of course." Make no mistake about it—through the meteoric rise from nightclubs and concerts to Broadway shows and television specials, Streisand's eyes were always set firmly on Hollywood stardom. For La Streisand, *stardom* meant *movie stardom*. Right off the bat. No carefully orchestrated plan of increasingly respectable roles, a cameo here, a supporting appearance there. Oh no.

> *Eyes on the target and wham—*
> *One shot, one gunshot and BAM!*

Oh yes.

Before the release of *Funny Girl,* Streisand's future in movies was actually an enormous question mark, and many Hollywood veterans predicted failure. There was the not-so-insignificant matter of her unusual looks: the large nose, the close-set, piercing blue eyes, the inch-long fingernails (grown, she claimed, to prevent fulfillment of her mother's wish that she become a typist or secretary). Barbra's looks were exotic enough to 1960s audiences in nightclubs and Broadway theaters, but in those milieus, she wasn't seen in Technicolor close-up.

In the darkened setting of a theater or concert hall, there was a remove. Yes, the one-woman television specials presented her front and center in sixty-minute formats replete with close-ups, but that was a much smaller screen and home viewing to boot—the audience could simply switch stations if they didn't like her. But on a fifty-foot silver screen? Would Columbia Pictures lose a fortune betting that the theater magic of the Brooklyn oddball could translate to the movies? The answer blew through Hollywood instantly; in Streisand's case *talent* was beauty, and with the premiere of *Funny Girl,* Streisand single-handedly changed the Hollywood standard of beauty. And thereby did nothing less than change how America defined beauty.

Barbra Streisand's first entrance in *Funny Girl*—her entrance into Hollywood itself—is actually the stuff of legend. Back to the audience, leopard-skin coat collar pulled high, she walks into the New Amsterdam Theater, her face not revealed until she looks into the mirror and self-deprecatingly murmurs, "Hello, gorgeous." She looks hurt, tears glistening in her eyes, and the audience is on her side without even knowing who she is or what her story is. Has there ever been a better star entrance on film? Certainly none has proven more effective.

Beautifully lit by master cinematographer Harry Stradling and directed by Hollywood legend William Wyler, Streisand turned in a performance of dazzling range. Comically detailed as she bemoans her fate in a voice of pure Brooklynese—"I'm a bagel on a plate full of onion rolls"—and launches into the Fanny/Barbra character-defining "I'm the Greatest Star." It's "I am" and "I need" time, which constitutes very important character definition in terms of musical film structure, and the song is here sung in a voice so true, so kaleidoscopic in its moods, that the viewer capitulates in this, her very first number. Hitting all of the bases, she is touching in her vulnerability as she sings "People," that yearning paean to love and fulfillment. Head tilted back, voice rising with mounting intensity, nasal emphasis for the key phrases—this is the very definition of yearning, and one only notices in passing that the song is sung on a clean and sparkling Lower East Side street that never existed anywhere but in the make-believe world of a Hollywood sound stage. Best of all, there is the defiant Fanny/Barbra as she explodes into the first-half capper "Don't Rain on My Parade." Magnificently staged by Herb Ross (who directed all of the film's musical sequences), the "Don't Rain on My Parade" sequence is Hollywood musical movie making at its finest. When Fanny's Ziegfeld Follies friends beg her not to follow Nicky Arnstein, the litany of *don'ts*—"Don't quit the Follies," "Don't go"—reaches a crescendo until Barbra's Fanny covers her ears and explodes into song with "Don't tell me not to live." The pulsating rhythm of Styne's melody, perfectly complemented by Bob Merrill's canny lyrics, propels Fanny forward as she runs for a train, then into a cab, and finally onto a tugboat, to reach Nicky Arnstein and grab her chance at love. Nothing could stop this force of nature, and by the time Barbra sails past the Statue of Liberty on a tugboat, flowers held aloft in an echo of Lady Liberty and her torch, it is the Statue of Liberty herself who has been upstaged.

Funny Girl is great fun in its first half, detailing the rags-to-riches show business climb of Fanny Brice. The audience experiences a sense of exhilaration watching Brooklyn native and Jewish oddball Barbra Streisand's real-life star being born, just as New York native and Jewish oddball Fanny Brice's is born onscreen. The film sags noticeably in the second half, the climb to the top always proving to be more fun in show biz Cinderella stories. Oftentimes the film's second half moves perilously close to soap opera, and suffers from both a lack of comedy (as Fanny's marriage deteriorates), and a lack of music (eight musical numbers before intermission, only four after, and just one of these—"My Man"—really lands). But throughout, Barbra never falters, working a taut comic speaking voice against a warm, lush singing voice. By the time of the "My Man" finale, all bets are off; lit only on her face

and hands, black dress against black background, tears rolling down her face after husband Nicky Arnstein has left her for good, Fanny/Barbra begins tremulously. Will she make it? One might as well ask if the sun will rise in the morning. Slowly gathering strength as the song builds, by the time Streisand powerfully leans into the second "Oh my man I love him so—he'll never know," the only audience reaction is one of total surrender. Not because of force of will, which was to happen in the future, but simply from sheer force of talent.

Funny Girl also set the template for the theme of over half of Streisand's movies: odd-looking girl falls in love with gorgeous guy, crises abound until the climactic moment when he all but smites his forehead and in an amazed tone says, "You *are* beautiful!" At its best, as in *Funny Girl* and *The Way We Were,* this theme reinforces the audience connection with Barbra—the underdog makes good. At its worst, as in *The Mirror Has*

"HELLO, GORGEOUS": FROM BROADWAY (1964) TO HOLLYWOOD (1968). SPRINGER/*PHOTOFEST,* *PHOTOFEST*

"I'M THE GREATEST STAR"—AND SHE WAS.
THE OSCAR-WINNING FILM DEBUT, *FUNNY GIRL,* 1968. *PHOTOFEST*

Two Faces, there is no sense of a character being portrayed. It is just Barbra Streisand forcing the audience to consider her beautiful, imposing her will while she continues to work out childhood issues. This is a particularly pointless battle, and has severely hampered her screen legacy, for the simple reason that it's a battle Streisand long ago won. It's as if she's the only one who doesn't realize the battle is over.

As a follow-up to *Funny Girl,* Streisand committed to film an even more successful Broadway musical, the wildly popular *Hello, Dolly!* The rapturous reception she received for *Funny Girl* bolstered the hopes of Twentieth Century Fox executives for the 1969 release of *Hello, Dolly!* There was just one problem: the twenty-seven-year-old Streisand was at least twenty years too young for the role. Even a casual viewer is left wondering "If she's widowed now, was she married at age nine?!" Her "middle-aged" matchmaker, Dolly Levi, appears to be younger than any of the characters she is helping to find mates.

Streisand herself has referred to *Dolly* as a mistake, but in truth that

A VERY YOUNG DOLLY LEVI DUETS WITH THE GREAT SATCHMO.
HELLO DOLLY!, 1969. *PHOTOFEST*

description is better saved for several of her other films. The movie itself, directed and choreographed, respectively, by musical screen legends Gene Kelly and Michael Kidd, works in fits and starts, and while Streisand's youth undercuts the premise of the entire film, the movie stops dead whenever she is offscreen, coming back to life only when she appears to drive the silly plot forward. She may be too young for the role, but she looks thoroughly at ease in the 1890s costumes and settings, and her musicianship remains impeccable. In fact, the movie exhibits the joyful sense of release associated with great musicals only when Streisand is singing: The newly written character-defining opening number "Just Leave Everything to Me," the muttered ad-libs in "Dancing," the sense of mutual fun and respect when singing the title song with the great Louis Armstrong—these high points compensate for the farcical story.

On the plus side of the ledger, there is first-class musical support from soon-to-be Broadway legend Tommy Tune as artist Ambrose Kemper, and several individual scenes hit the bullseye: Barbra's high-octane comic attack as she manipulates Horace Vandergelder into marriage in the dining sequence after the title song is great fun, while her exuberant vocal on "So Long Dearie," wherein she pokes fun at her own energy, provides the film with a genuinely great musical sequence. These are enough—but barely—to compensate for the ridiculous cardboard secondary characters that so damage the film. The talented Michael Crawford plays Vandergelder's chief clerk, Cornelius Hackl, not so much as a naïf, but as an imbecile. He is irritating in the extreme, and the viewer cannot imagine hatmaker Irene Molloy (Marianne McAndrew) taking him seriously for even one minute. It is no accident that their two solo songs, "Ribbons Down My Back" and "It Only Takes a Moment," bring the film to a grinding halt.

As a film, *Dolly* is a case of "too much": too much Michael Kidd choreography in "Dancing" and too much of the frantic waiter's ballet leading up to the title tune. Kelly, a movie musical great who proved himself a gifted director on *On The Town* and *Singin' in the Rain,* and Kidd, who choreographed the terrific numbers in *Seven Brides for Seven Brothers,* make little use of the widescreen possibilities (contrast this with Wyler and Ross on *Funny Girl*), doing little more than shovelling more and more bodies on screen with no apparent purpose. Worst of all, this mistaken philosophy of "more is more" overwhelms the slender, farcical story and throws the film out of balance. There are too many people in the Act I closer "Before the Parade Passes By." In fact, nothing in that elephantine production number— none of the thousands of marchers or brass bands—matches the sheer power and excitement of Streisand's solo vocal as she wills herself back to life. As Barbra/Dolly eagerly rushes forward, singing of her determination to rejoin the human race, the audience experiences a real sense of excitement. Unfortunately, it is an excitement which deflates and lies inert when confronted with the lumbering, overly literal depiction of the parade. Streisand may be too young for the part, searching here (a Mae West–inflected comic delivery) and there (an ironic approach to the more ridiculous plot elements) in an attempt to center her character. Nonetheless, there is, in the end, a musicality, a sense of Streisand herself having fun and not taking herself too seriously, which is sorely lacking in all of her films from 1976's *A Star is Born* until 2004's *Meet the Fockers.*

Talent such as hers will not break when tested; it becomes enriched.
—Vincent Canby in his *New York Times* review of *On a Clear Day,*
June 18, 1970

Streisand's last movie contracted for before she had even arrived in Hollywood was Lerner and Lane's *On a Clear Day You Can See Forever.* Barbra herself chose the gifted Vincente Minnelli as director, based upon her admiration for his award-winning films *An American in Paris* and *Gigi.* The resulting film of *Clear Day* proved to be schizophrenic in structure and quality, hopscotching between 1970 New York City and 19th-century England. In fact, the film actually remains emblematic of Streisand's entire film career: moments of brilliance mixed with thoughts of "if only."

Playing Daisy Gamble, a modern-day nonmatriculated college-age student in New York who regresses to a previous life in nineteenth-century England under hypnosis from Dr. Marc Chabot (Yves Montand), Streisand, ironically, overplays her first modern character. Throughout the present-day sequences she appears shrill, her arms flailing wildly and widely, and she is ludicrously overdressed for a college student; in those days of student revolutionaries and early feminism, how many female college students wore couture clothes to class and sported matching hats to complete the ensemble? Similarly, she falls victim to a design scheme that places her in a classroom setting that surely exists only in the imagination of a Hollywood set designer, not to mention a not-on-this-planet's professor's office occupying two floors connected by a circular staircase. These laughable settings are topped by Daisy's own apartment: With no apparent means of sup-

BUDDING DIRECTOR—THE GLEAM IN HER EYE SAYS IT ALL. ON THE SET OF *ON A CLEAR DAY YOU CAN SEE FOREVER,* 1970. *PHOTOFEST*

port, she seems to live in a New York City apartment that features a football-stadium-sized rooftop garden. Such out-of-whack physical production values only serve to heighten a sense of unreality and show how out of touch the Hollywood studios, and by extension the movie musicals, were in the face of changing audience tastes.

At the same time, the film is structured in a peculiar manner for a musical and leads an audience to feel uncertain as to what exactly they are watching. Is it a comedy? A musical? Billed as a Barbra Streisand musical, there is only one song in the first thirty-two minutes of the film, and the third song does not occur until the fifty-six-minute mark.

The modern-day sequences are not completely without merit; Barbra can clearly still wisecrack with the best of them, adding unexpected line readings such as her reluctant admission, "I make flowers grow." However, the Brooklyn schtick is here unrelenting, a fact underscored when her incessant whining is immediately followed by the warm lush singing voice she employs in song. This contrast is here thrown into stark relief; it is as if the Yiddish-inflected speaking voice is counterbalanced by the perfect almost WASPy diction and timbre of her singing voice. Is this the same girl? Turns out she's not, because Daisy is a girl who has seen and done it all before—many times in many lives.

And it is in the ensuing flashbacks to Daisy's previous life in the nineteenth century as Melinda Tentrees that Barbra and director Minnelli soar together. He, clearly more at home in Regency England than in the grubby New York of 1970, presents Streisand as a pure Hollywood star. She does look "beautiful" in the opulent clothes, and he elicits a comic performance from her that ranks amongst her best work onscreen. Speaking and walking at half of the speed she employs in the modern-day sequences, Barbra and the audience relax together and the film takes off. Employing a broad yet believable cockney accent that evolves into posh upper-crust speech as she ascends the social ranks, Streisand exudes a delicious sense of fun without ever overplaying. Certainly she has never been presented to better physical advantage on film than when she sings "Love with All the Trimmings" in voice-over. Seducing her handsome young lover (John Richardson) with highly sensual glances over a full-course, high-society banquet, making her goblet of wine a sexual object, Barbra is the dazzler she always dreamed of being. It is with a real sense of irritation that the viewer is brought back to the present-day New York portion of the story, a shortcoming not helped by the notable lack of chemistry between Streisand and co-star Yves Montand.

Highly trimmed in the editing process, the film's coherence suffers as a result ("Quick—was that Jack Nicholson who just flashed by as Streisand's step-brother?!") Perhaps changing musical tastes caused there to be only eight songs in the entire production, but not only did the film not do well at the box office, the soundtrack did not even break the top 100 on the charts. Faced with this relative lack of success, Streisand knew it was time for a change. No more old-fashioned studio musicals, no more unreality. Just as she was tentatively exploring rock music in her recording career, she was determined to present herself on film as a woman of today. With her next film—her first nonmusical—she brought herself smack dab into the true reality of 1970.

The Owl and the Pussycat, based on a slight Broadway play by Bill Manhoff, presented a new Barbra, a present-day Barbra. Playing a prostitute who

DORIS WILGUS, MODELING HER TRAFFIC-STOPPING "EXPENSIVE CREATION." *THE OWL AND THE PUSSYCAT,* 1970. *PHOTOFEST*

modeled form-fitting nightgowns that, according to co-star George Segal's character Felix, "came in a plain brown wrapper," Streisand seemed liberated to be playing a woman in real-life, grungy New York City. Directed by Herb Ross and filmed on location in New York, the film is interesting to view in light of its status as Streisand's first nonmusical role on film. She seems free—looser—and unlike in *The Main Event,* here the lingering shots of Barbra's legs and rear end make sense (not to mention that the diva looks pretty damn good). Doris Waverly is a prostitute and since the "plain brown wrapper" nightgown features hands on the breasts, a heart at the crotch, and "Doris" embroidered on her posterior, shots of her body actually help tell us about the character. Similarly, so do the gum snapping and the strident voice rising to an interborough screech. The Brooklyn accent is stretched to the breaking point, but never topples into caricature. George Segal and Barbra play off each other beautifully, his prissy would-be author matching her brassy dame every step of the way. Eying her vaguely pornographic nightgown and contemptuous of her claim to be a model, Felix (Segal) asks: "For whom do you model—the Boston Strangler?" Retorts Doris: "Listen, Mr. Sherman. If you're lucky I'll let you try it on." (It's interesting to note how many times Streisand's Doris refers to Segal's Felix as a "fag," a term repeated in *Up the Sandbox*. Ah, *tempus fugit*. When the film is viewed today, so strong is the viewer's awareness of Streisand's real-life liberal political beliefs that upon hearing these insults, one's first reaction inevitably is that feminist and gay-rights advocate Streisand would never countenance that slur today). Until the film sags in the last twenty minutes, the stars make a great team, and like Streisand-and-Redford, Streisand-and-Segal is a pairing that should have been repeated (in *The Mirror Has Two Faces* they did not play opposite each other, and almost literally did not interact).

Audiences responded favorably, making the film a success at the box office. Critical response was mostly favorable, with Pauline Kael, a particularly strong champion of Barbra's in the early films, writing in *The New Yorker* that Streisand "makes her lines funny musically and she can wring more changes on a line than anybody since W.C. Fields, who was also a master of inflection." Conversely, Vincent Canby in *The New York Times* opined that casting Barbra in a straight comedy would rank in any compilation of the modern world's ten most unrewarding stunts, "close to Charles A. Stephens's 1920 attempt to ride over Niagara Falls in a barrel, which turned out to be a fatal mistake."

The film achieved a certain notoriety for Streisand's first nude scene (stills of which ended up in the adult magazine *High Society,* until Streisand sued to prevent copies being distributed). In typical Streisand fashion, she first froze at the prospect of filming a topless scene ("What would my mother think?"), but after finally relenting and undertaking the scene, demanded that it be filmed a second time because she felt sure that she could improve upon her performance. In a similarly typical fashion, the film contained what was already becoming the standard scene between Barbra and her leading man: Together they discuss whether she really is beautiful and—surprise, surprise—they both agree that she is. . . .

The *Owl and the Pussycat* did indeed make Barbra's screen image appear younger, and restored her to box office favor after stumbling with *Clear Day*. Her next film, *What's Up, Doc?* continued to present her in a youthful, natural fashion, and the film, director Peter Bogdanovich's tribute to screwball comedies, proved a smash at the box office, breaking records at Radio City Music Hall, somewhat to Streisand's surprise. Ironically, the film was an almost completely re-worked version of a film entitled *A Glimpse of Tiger* which had been intended as a vehicle for ex-husband Elliot Gould, and throughout filming, Streisand apparently expressed doubts about the material. Yet none of the doubts show onscreen—tan, with long blonde hair framing her face, Barbra appears to be having genuine fun.

The film centers around the mix-up of four identical red plaid suitcases, and spins off in different directions at a dizzying pace, always propelled by the antics of Streisand's character, the film's heroine, Judy Maxwell. Judy has seemingly attended twenty different colleges with twenty different majors thus far, and her relentless pursuit of stuffy musicologist Howard Bannister (Ryan O'Neal, never better onscreen than in this tribute to Cary Grant) works precisely because the viewer knows he has absolutely no chance of resisting Judy. Hilarious complications ensue in the person of Howard's frumpy and repressed fiancée, beautifully played by Madeline Kahn (in one memorable image she is seen looking nauseous as she reads *The Sensuous Woman*). Best of

**AN INSPIRED COMIC PERFORMANCE
IN *WHAT'S UP, DOC?*, 1972. PHOTOFEST**

all, there is a particularly lovely moment when the reclining Streisand serenades object of her affection Ryan O'Neal with a limpid version of "As Time Goes By," complete with unexpected pratfall mid-song. Great entertainment, pure and simple.

The pratfalls and outrageous situations inherent in a screwball comedy unfold herein with their own perfectly demented logic, effortlessly dominated by a Streisand who is so attractive and relaxed that she almost glows. Barbra/Judy may be the aggressor who instigates all of the action, but she never does it abrasively. This girl is so much fun that you root for her every step of the way. Howard Bannister would be an idiot to turn down Judy Maxwell, and when the film ends with Barbra's exuberant, joy-filled rendition of Cole Porter's "You're the Top" over the credits, the audience exits glowing almost as much as the star.

At this point, Streisand really was America's funny girl. Hollywood stardom firmly assured, she sought to gain increased control over her

films, and along with Paul Newman, Sidney Poitier, and Steve Mc-
Queen, formed First Artists Production Company, Ltd., hoping to
thereby exercise this greater control over projects about which she
cared deeply. It was such thinking that led her to make one of the
strangest films of her career, *Up the Sandbox,* the first of three films
that comprise a category one could call, "Oy vey, what was she thinking?"

Up the Sandbox, a film which Streisand regards highly to this day, is
stuffed with so many ideas that it oftentimes feels like four movies in
one: Feminism, radical politics, mother-daughter relationships, and a
woman's right to choose are all depicted in under two hours.
Streisand, playing WASPy housewife Margaret Reynolds, actually
turns in an excellent performance, and an argument could even be
fashioned claiming it to be her most consistent performance. Certainly, it contains her most low-key acting, totally devoid of mannerism and schtick.

The believable tone is set right from the start with the opening
sequence showing Margaret bathing her children. *Up the Sandbox,*
Streisand's sixth movie, is the first to show her interacting with children, and her naturalism is a welcome sign. In fact, all of the sequences
depicting Margaret's "real" life with her college professor husband,
Paul (David Selby), play well. Two scenes of mother-daughter conflict
(propelled by an excellent portrayal of Margaret's mother by Jane
Hoffman, a portrayal with echoes of Streisand's real-life mother-
daughter relationship that is more fully explored in *The Mirror Has Two
Faces*) register particularly strongly. As Margaret grapples with the idea
of an abortion after discovering that she is pregnant with a third child,
the viewer gains a real sense of a modern woman trying to balance her
own needs with those of her family.

The problem with the film, and it is ultimately an insurmountable
one, is that the fantasy sequences wherein Margaret expresses her innermost desires and fears are unclear, attenuated, and bring the film to a

standstill each time they occur. There are six of them, and while the first, Margaret's take on the idea of her husband having an affair, is somewhat amusing, the second, involving a Castro figure who is really a woman complete with fake beard and breasts, is interminable and static. It is no help that this fantasy, and the subsequent one depicting Margaret and black militants blowing up the Statue of Liberty, are dimly lit to the point that the action within the Statue is often indecipherable. The real-life sequences at first re-engage the viewer after each fantasy scene, but by the time of the sixth fantasy (the abortion sequence), the viewer, having been jerked back and forth for ninety minutes, likely will find him- or herself not really caring. *Up the Sandbox* explores important and pertinent issues, albeit complete with what is now jarringly anachronistic dialogue (Margaret uses the term "fag" and introduces herself as "Mrs. Paul Reynolds"). The fantasy sequences, which should lift the film, actually sink it, and thirty years after its release, the film remains an interesting failure. The audience simply cannot connect in any meaningful way with the skim-the-surface-of-every-topic nature of the film.

Writing in *The New Yorker,* Pauline Kael described the film as a "joyful mess" and the film proved a dud at the box office. This commercial failure was forgotten upon the 1973 release of *The Way We Were.* Propelled by a #1 title song, and the best acting reviews Streisand was ever to receive in her film career, *The Way We Were* proved a box office bonanza, and provided her with the role and image which resonated most clearly not only with her loyal fans, but also with a new audience embracing this old-fashioned love story.

Written by Arthur Laurents, the librettist and director of *I Can Get It For You Wholesale, The Way We Were* provided Streisand with that once-in-a-lifetime opportunity which defines true movie stardom: the chance to play an idealized version of herself and thereby cement permanent fan identification. After all, true movie stars, as opposed to actors, portray different aspects of their same essential self in film after film. *The Way We Were* centered on a love story of opposites attracting: loudmouthed ugly duckling political activist Katie Morosky—a character with attributes the audience felt Streisand personally embodied—falls for, in the words of Laurents's screenplay, a "gorgeous goyishe guy" (Hubbell Gardiner), played by Robert Redford, and wins him through sheer force of personality. (Laurents largely based the character of Katie Morosky upon a college friend named, ironically enough, Fanny Price.) Ranging from 1930s college life to the 1950s ban-the-bomb movement, the film struck a chord in the archetypal Streisand fashion, resonating with every girl who felt herself to be ugly, with every gay boy who felt totally left out, with every *person* who ever felt that their true, smart, attractive personality went totally unrecognized. Beyond the core audience, however, the impossibility of a happy ending for two such star-crossed lovers also resonated with a broad cross-section of the American public, with all those whose personal lives left them frustrated, confused, and bursting with unspoken passion. This was the film for Streisand fans and nonfans alike.

Director Sydney Pollack and screenwriter Laurents set up the film in such a canny fashion that the viewer is seduced before even realizing it. Opening in New York City during the years of World War II, Katie's political activism is instantly established during the opening sequence at a radio broadcast, and when she subsequently spots a drunken Hubbell at the El Morocco nightclub, tenderly brushing the hair off his forehead in a gesture famously repeated in the closing sequence, the film seamlessly glides back to their 1930s college days. As the bittersweet title tune fills the soundtrack over images of crew races and track meets, all filmed in golden sunshine, the normally cynical viewer forgets to ask if any college days were ever so halcyon. Then again, there's no need to do so, because the title tune asks the question for the viewer: "Was it all so simple then? Or has time rewritten every line?"

Streisand connected with the material not only because of her affinity for and with Katie Morosky, but also because the themes of politics in 1950s America mirrored her own growing outspoken political activism on behalf of the Democratic Party. Laurents's merging of love story and political background gave the movie a texture and richness missing from most movie love stories, and the conflicted lovers actually speak as they would in real life:

Hubbell: "You push too hard. Every damn minute."

Katie: "I want you to be better . . . until you're every wonderful thing you should be and will be."

The attraction and difficulties between these lovers makes sense. Audiences even saw reflections of America's own personality in the characters of Katie Morosky and Redford's golden boy character, Hubbell Gardner. If Redford/Gardiner, in the words of the screenplay, was "Like the country he lived in—everything came too easily to him" (words Laurents smartly follows up with "but at least he knew it. About once a month he worried that he was a fraud . . ."), then Streisand/Morosky represented the better half of that country—demanding better, pushing for a more egalitarian society.

In *The Way We Were* Barbra Streisand delivers the most consistent, fully realized screen acting of her career. Katie Morosky's abrasive exterior, which hides a mile-wide streak of vulnerability, is instantly established, as is Katie's changing relationship with Hubbell; from lovestruck college student to married life both blissful and painful, culminating in a final disillusioned yet still loving reaction to Hubbell—this is a multi-layered characterization expertly laid out in Laurents's screenplay and beautifully delivered by Streisand. There are no mannerisms, no characterizations through personality, just a fully crafted performance, which impressed upon the viewer just how much Streisand was capable of as an actress (and which also serves to underscore the waste inherent in nonsense like *For Pete's Sake* and *The Main Event*).

It is no accident that every one of Streisand's first-rate performances has come with an acclaimed, top-tier director at the helm: William Wyler—*Funny Girl,* Vincente Minnelli—(past sequences) *On a Clear Day,* Peter Bogdanovich—*What's Up, Doc?,* Sydney Pollack—*The Way We Were,* and Martin Ritt—*Nuts.* These skilled directors enhance the Streisand abilities, just as singing with a Judy Garland or Louis Armstrong elevates

MISMATCHED LOVERS—AND BARBRA'S BEST PERFORMANCE.
THE WAY WE WERE, 1973. PHOTOFEST

her vocals. Given a lesser director, Barbra can often upstage the material through sheer force of personality, serving neither herself nor the film.

Streisand rode the wave of her excellent reviews to a second Academy Award nomination as best actress, and although favored (along with Joanne Woodward for *Summer Wishes, Winter Dreams*) to win the award, she lost to Glenda Jackson in the lightweight comedy *A Touch of Class.* While *A Touch of Class* has been largely forgotten, *The Way We Were,* thirty years after its release, remains a cultural touchstone, sometimes revered, sometimes parodied and mocked. It is a film that inspires cultural references in films as diverse as the female bonding movie *Boys on the Side* and the gay-themed cable television series *Queer as Folk*.

For years there has been talk of a sequel to *The Way We Were*, one that would revisit the characters decades later, and Laurents in fact wrote a full treatment of such a script, but plans have failed to materialize. In an odd way, Streisand's fans are almost happier to freeze their "memories" with the end of the film: Katie and Hubbell, fleetingly reunited in front of New York City's Plaza Hotel, Katie lovingly brushing the hair out of his eyes, still in love and realizing it's impossible, as the camera pulls back and the yearning title tune fills the soundtrack . . .

After the triumph of *The Way We Were*, Barbra had her choice of any film she wanted to make. She was the #1 female movie star, the #1 female recording artist, she could film virtually any script she liked—and she blew it. Squandered the opportunity on a meaningless piece of fluff called *For Pete's Sake* (exhibit #2 in the "Oy vey, what was she thinking?" listing of her films).

It's not that *For Pete's Sake* was offensively bad—it's too innocuous for that. The real problem is that Streisand's participation in the film was pointless, and while there is still a lightness to her comic performances at this stage of her career, it is still several steps backwards from the inspired lunacy of *What's Up, Doc?* and *The Owl and the Pussycat*. Written and co-produced by Stanley Shapiro, who gained fame writing the Doris Day-Rock Hudson comedies, *For Pete's Sake* feels and plays like a second-rate, fifteen-years-too-late imitation of those comedies. After a somewhat humorous set-up establishing that Henrietta and Pete Robbins (Streisand and Michael Sarrazin) are facing a severe cash-flow crisis, the second half of the film degenerates into increasingly unfunny scenes of slapstick adventures meant to solve these financial problems.

In reality, Barbra doesn't turn in a bad performance; she still scores with a wisecrack at the expense of her obnoxious sister-in-law (Estelle Parsons), and in an interesting reversal of 1970s Hollywood norms, the female lead (Streisand) drives the movie, both physically and verbally, while her male counterpart (Sarrazin) is reduced to the role of passive onlooker. This does not, however, overcome the fact that thousands of actresses could have played this role of a housewife struggling to help her husband by embarking on a series of wacky adventures. Streisand the feminist portraying a housewife who considers prostitution (albeit comically) to help her husband?! Barbra Streisand as a cattle rustler? It's a film that evaporates from memory the second it is over, and the biggest star in the world had laughs stolen from her by both the African American maid who refuses to do most of her work (Vivian Bonnell), and the cute Yiddishe madam played by Molly Picon.

The real damage to Streisand's reputation lay in the fact that for the first time there was widespread questioning of her claims of being a serious artist. After *The Way We Were*, for which even Streisand detractors grudgingly gave her credit, no one took *For Pete's Sake* seriously, except for the die-hard fans who showed up in large enough numbers to make the film a financial success. The actress who longed to play Juliet and L'Aiglon was now wearing long blonde wigs, floppy red hats, and riding cattle in the streets of New York City. She was trapped by her own stardom, and by now the kooky, cutting-edge singer/actress had fully morphed into the complacent bland queen of Hollywood studio fare.

BLAZING TONSILS

—Headline for Jay Cocks' *Time* magazine review of *Funny Lady*, March 21, 1975

If squandered capital was not exactly recouped with the 1975 release of *Funny Lady*, this sequel to Streisand's signature role of Fanny Brice did prove a box office bonanza, spawning a hit soundtrack and a last-ditch gasp of glory for the old-fashioned movie musical. Initially reluctant to film any sequel, let alone one to her greatest hit, Streisand was contractually obligated to producer Ray Stark for one more film. She rationalized her decision to undertake the sequel by stating that she found herself drawn to the script by Jay Presson Allen and Arnold Schulman because "what the script is about is losing one's fantasies and illusions and getting in touch with and appreciating reality." The resulting film? A very uneven big-budget behemoth of a movie.

As a film, *Funny Lady* moves in fits and starts, lumbering along at a stolid pace until Streisand electrifies it from time to time with a solo number. On the plus side, with James Caan playing Brice's second husband, Billy Rose, the co-stars' chemistry is actually quite good and Streisand and Caan, both of whom are good with a wisecrack, deliver their dialogue at a fitting *rat-a-tat-tat* speed. If Redford's pairing with Barbra worked because his cool reserve complemented her intensity, then Caan's co-starring performance works because he battles her for every inch of screen space. Billy Rose and Fanny Brice are both streetwise New Yorkers, as are Streisand and Caan, and Fanny's veneer of sophistication clashes very nicely with Caan's appropriate nervous energy as the feisty Rose. Never mind that Caan is taller and more handsome than the real-life Rose—the pairing works, as is made clear from the snappy dialogue heard when they first join forces:

Fanny: "If we hate the same people and you get your suit cleaned, it's a match."

The return to playing Fanny Brice is a comfortable one for Streisand. Physically she looks great in the lavish Bob Mackie/Ray Aghayan clothes, and unlike many modern-day stars in period pieces, she appears thoroughly at ease. This is clearly a woman who spent a lot of time in front of a mirror playing "let's pretend" as a little girl, because it is that sort of make-believe that informs fantasies of old-fashioned

Hollywood stardom, stardom complete with an every-hair-in-place-and-gorgeous-gowns kind of glamour. In addition, Barbra is beautifully lit and shot by master cinematographer James Wong Howe, with the movie beginning and ending with rather startling close-ups of her blue eyes.

In *Funny Lady* Streisand presents a much tougher Fanny Brice than she did in *Funny Girl*. It would be interesting to know the reaction of Fran and Ray Stark (Brice's daughter and son-in-law) to this different characterization, but it makes sense in the context of the film. Fanny is an older woman by now, and at times the film actually presents an adult love story with ups, downs, and even wit—no easy feat in a musical. Fanny and Billy seem like real people, and funny ones at that, as they bicker about the disastrous tryout of the show *Crazy Quilt:*

Billy: (referring to having borrowed money from the mob to finance the show) They're gonna build me into the West Side Highway.

Fanny: That's the only good news I've heard tonight.

Billy: I'm not kidding.

Fanny: Neither am I.

If, as Fanny says, she fell "in like" with Billy, that dynamic actually comes across on screen.

Musically, there are several terrific solo Streisand sequences. She is in great voice recording the period standard "More Than You Know," and the new Kander and Ebb ballad "Isn't This Better?" scores as both a first-rate ballad and a character-defining song.

Why then, does the film only succeed in bits and pieces? First (or last) there is an unfortunate tacked-on ending about a possible Billy and Fanny work reunion which makes the last ten minutes feel flabby, and which is nonmusical to boot. Ironically, however, the biggest reason for the film's unevenness is the staging of the musical numbers by director Herb Ross. The irony lies in the fact that Ross's first-rate staging of the musical numbers in *Funny Girl* proved a major reason for that film's success; in *Funny Lady*, however, he makes a crucial mistake which nearly undercuts all musical effectiveness except for some of the solo numbers. Wanting to achieve realism, he stages all of the numbers on an actual theatrical stage—no expansive sound-stage setting allowed. The resulting production numbers exude a cramped, claustrophobic feeling, and while Streisand's vocals soar on classics such as "Great Day," she looks uncomfortable standing center stage in that number, trying to avoid the chorus dancers careening all too closely to her. The resulting number feels nothing so much as lifeless. Ben Vereen's faux Fosse number "Clap Hands: Here Comes Charlie," complete with bowlers and white gloves, proves more gymnastic than memorable. The backstage sequences may be appropriately atmospheric, but the humor of watching an onstage disaster, herein depicted as *Crazy Quilt* unravels, was conveyed more succinctly and humorously by Ross himself in the "Roller Skate Rag" number in *Funny Girl.*

Similarly, "Let's Hear It For Me," the brassy Kander and Ebb tune meant to echo the force of "Don't Rain on My Parade," has a powerful driving vocal, but the effect is negated by the staging: As Streisand drives a car and flies in a bi-plane to reach Billy Rose, one realizes that the vehicles are moving, but Fanny Brice herself is basically stationary. There is no sense of the release that great musical numbers provide. Rather than exhilaration, the viewer feels something akin to detachment, idly contemplating the barely suppressed look of terror on Streisand's face as she drives her antique Rolls Royce at a speed which appears to peak at four miles per hour.

There is, however, one moment of sheer movie magic which reminds everyone watching just why La Streisand sits at the top of the heap. Alone on a darkened stage, having just found out that true love Nicky Arnstein has married another woman, Barbra as Fanny bitterly inverts the cheery sentiments of her latest recording, "How Lucky Can You Get." Giving full vent to her sarcasm and mocking self-loathing, Fanny/Barbra sings, "Gee—Whee—Wow—How lucky—How lucky can you get?" as she sets the solitary overhead light spinning wildly and stalks offstage. It is an Act I closer par excellence, more powerful than a chorus of hundreds, because it is filled with genuine human emotion. Astaire dancing solo, Streisand singing solo—this is the essence of movie stardom.

Critical reaction to the film was mixed to favorable, with the negative reviews harping on the fact that Streisand was revisiting overly familiar territory (in her *Village Voice* review, Molly Haskell sarcastically queried, "Will there be a *Funny Granny*?") Interestingly, Barbra's chief critical cheerleader, Pauline Kael, wrote an unusually vitriolic review in the *New Yorker*, repelled by a performance she felt resembled a female impersonator's impression of Barbra Streisand. In an across-the-board swipe, Kael opined that "You can see the moviemakers weren't just going to make a movie—they were going to kill us. That's the thinking that has all but destroyed the American musical and it may destroy Barbra Streisand too."

The positive reviews outweighed the negative, however, and while *Funny Lady* broke no new ground, it recouped some of the standing lost with *For Pete's Sake* and served to cement Barbra's hold on the box office. In an era of stars who pretended to be just folks, Streisand made no such attempt. She lived the life of a movie star, ensconced in a gated mansion, granting no interviews, giving no concerts, and all the time actually increasing her allure, the unobtainable becoming that much more desirable and fascinating. A lifetime of yearning for stardom was not about to be undercut by accessibility. If old-time Hollywood royalty like Garbo and Hepburn were remote, then she would be too. Barbra genuinely wanted to be left alone, and together with manager Martin Erlichman planned a successful campaign to maintain

THE ULTIMATE DIVA MOMENT—"HOW LUCKY CAN YOU GET?"
FUNNY LADY, 1975. PHOTOFEST

her stardom and increase her allure by her very remoteness. It wouldn't have succeeded without her extraordinary talent to back it up, but with all the cunning and stratagems of four-star generals, they made it work.

At this point, Streisand could do no wrong for the studios financially, and her fan base continued to grow. Increasingly outspoken, however, about not being able to control her own films, and frustrated by the male-dominated world of Hollywood, Streisand, with hairdresser-turned-boyfriend-and-producer Jon Peters firmly controlling her professional life, announced plans to star in and executive produce a rock-music version of the thrice filmed Hollywood classic *A Star Is Born*. The result of the announcement: all hell breaking loose, and an avalanche of (mostly bad) press which could be summed up in one simple sentiment: "How dare she?" Hollywood may have been perceived as a liberal town, but the powers that be did not want their hegemony challenged by a mere actress, no matter how popular. It was

**UNEXPECTEDLY SINGING LIVE TO QUIET THE CROWD OF 55,000
DURING FILMING OF *A STAR IS BORN,* 1976. *CORBIS***

also interesting to note that although Streisand was granted a grudging respect for her success and box office clout, she was not liked within the Hollywood community, primarily because of her independence. She broke the rules, insisted on doing things her own way, wouldn't cooperate with the press, and still triumphed with the public. Such unpopularity very possibly cost her the Oscar for *The Way We Were.* More important, it made Hollywood insiders eager for Streisand to fail—schadenfreude writ large.

With the feminist movement in full cry, Streisand once again fit the zeitgeist of the time. She would star, write songs, design her wardrobe, and produce the whole damn shooting match on *A Star Is Born,* and no man would tell her no. No man *could* tell her no. Streisand's gay fans applauded her resolution in breaking down barriers, feminists cheered her on—and the press got ready to pounce.

Nothing in Streisand's career to that point could have fully prepared her for the beating she took as soon as filming started. The press gleefully reported the fight between Peters and leading man Kris Kristofferson, a disagreement which degenerated into an obscenity-laced screaming match picked up on open microphones before a stadium full of fifty-five thousand fans assembled for a concert sequence. The press couldn't seem to decide whom they liked to belittle more: Jon Peters for being a loud abrasive streetfighter, a hairdresser-turned-producer who had the audacity to think he knew anything about filmmaking, or Streisand for thinking a woman could successfully fill multiple creative roles. Who did she think she was—Orson Welles? The deepest wound of all for Streisand came with the pre-release publication in *New West* Magazine of director Frank Pierson's lengthy account of his "Battles with Barbra and Jon." Streisand felt that the director-actor bond had been totally violated, and in her lengthy *Playboy* Magazine interview (cover story, October 1977), likened her resulting feelings to the Edvard Munch painting "The Scream."

> *Barbra sings to make you forget tension, worry, uncertainty;*
> *she soars above it all. You feel excited and wonderful.*
> *She throws it away as though it were a gift not worth having.*
> —Frank Pierson, Director, *A Star Is Born*

The publicity reached epic proportions—after all, this was a Hollywood classic about Hollywood itself, newly reinvented by the town's biggest female star and her Johnny-come-lately boyfriend, with filming marked by public battles and denunciations. All of the hype peaked in the Barbara Walters special interview with Streisand on the eve of release. For this interview, Streisand "shared" the interview hour with no less a personage than newly elected President Jimmy Carter, with Barbra demanding—and receiving—an unprecedented first rush approval of the interview footage. Never one to shy away from the grand gesture, Streisand planned the release for Christmas

Day 1976. Christmas day arrived, the film unspooled around the country, and—

And the result was an artistic disaster. It wasn't just that the reviews were scathing, though they were—"A BORE IS STARRED" was among the kinder review headlines. It's that the critics seemed to spend as much time reviewing Barbra's perceived megalomania and personal life with Peters as they did the film. For years now, Streisand, the biggest star in town, had been inaccessible to the press. All interview requests were turned down. There were no concert tours, no television appearances to hype the latest movie or album, Streisand in effect saying "I don't need you." Now it was time for payback.

The press responded by turning on Streisand and the film closest to her heart. Streisand was pushing back the barriers for women in Hollywood and she was resented for that very fact by the press. Just as in the beginning of her career, the question was "Who does she think she is?" In the press's overkill, they overlooked one central fact: The movie was so terrible that it spoke for itself, with no overkill needed.

Never before or since had Streisand stumbled so far off the road. Sporting an unattractive, red-tinted curly hairdo and repeatedly wearing unflattering 1970s men's suits as a means of commenting on the roles imposed on women by society, Streisand barrels through the film playing a totally unbelievable rock star on the rise named Esther Hoffman Howard. The viewer is beaten over the head with Streisand's comments about gender roles, and co-star Kris Kristofferson, playing John Norman Howard, a rock star on his way down, is not spared either. When Esther and John Norman Howard first make love, Esther is on top. She affixes jeweled eyebrows and rouge to his face, and it is Esther who proposes marriage to him. Streisand, who has always spoken of trusting the audience, here seems not to believe that the audience will pick up her "message" unless it is repeated over and over again.

Perhaps—and somewhat understandably so—the endless battles Streisand had to fight as a woman in Hollywood in order to produce the film and control her own destiny simply carried over too strongly into her characterization in the film. Nevertheless and unfortunately, all of the pathos present in the 1937 and 1954 versions, starring Janet Gaynor and Judy Garland, respectively, was lost, or rather trampled. This Esther Hoffman Howard is not in the least vulnerable. She is one tough cookie—a steely woman who would have demanded stardom and success; when she tells John Norman Howard, "Listen, I can take all the tenderness you have," she appears to be so self-sufficient and aggressive that the words are nearly laughable. Her "star is born" at a Native American benefit concert, because John Norman unexpectedly introduces her and forces her to perform. Esther claims to be scared and unprepared but in Streisand's Mack-truck performance, Esther's actions as she "nervously" heads to the stage all but say, "It's about time. Out of my way—I'm due center stage." Even more damaging, Streisand, the last of the great romantic Tin Pan Alley songbirds, simply bears no relationship to a true rock star. Janis Joplin she wasn't. (Bette Midler, an actress who eventually hurt her own film career through poor choices, made a far more convincing rock star in her terrific performance as the Joplin-like title character in *The Rose*). Streisand's perfect enunciation, seamless legato, manicured nails, and excessive, detailed backlighting did not a rock star make.

Overly cutesy in both mannerism and dialogue (to John Norman: "I'll be your groupie if you'll be mine"), at times Streisand is downright grating. Kristofferson is actually much more at home in the rock world milieu, and at times is touching in his portrayal of a burned-out rock star who has seen the bottom of too many bottles and can't stop his own slide towards total self-destruction. Unfortunately, unlike the '37 and '54 versions of the story, there is absolutely no common ground for these characters to inhabit. Why they were so wildly attracted to each other remains a total mystery.

The highly popular score was actually a mishmash of pseudo-rock, ballads, and patter songs, contributed by many composers, several of

ESTHER HOFFMAN HOWARD—ONE TOUGH COOKIE. *A STAR IS BORN,* 1976. *PHOTOFEST*

whom were totally unsuited for the rock milieu. ASCAP stalwarts Marilyn and Alan Bergman writing for a supposed rock musical?! At the most basic musical level, no one seemed to analyze the fact that rock music is about raw primal energy, not pithy wordplay.

The screenplay by Joan Didion and John Gregory Dunne is a lackluster updating of golden era Hollywood to the anything goes world of pop music in the 1970s. The stakes don't seem as high, and the screenplay is littered with inaccuracies. Just one example: When Esther (Streisand) and the Oreos (her two black backup singers played by Clydie King and Vanetta Fields) are fired from a jingle recording session about cat food because Esther can't stop laughing, Esther simply says "I'm sorry girls—I'm allergic to cats anyway." The Oreos' response? They nod, understanding, and kiss her. It seemingly didn't occur to the filmmakers that a true-to-life response would have shown the Oreos saying, "Yeah? Well get your ass back to that microphone because there's money on the line here."

There is exactly one extended sequence which works well—the

one wherein Esther's star is born as she sings "I Believe in Love" and "Woman in the Moon" at a benefit concert. Yes, the two songs are pop, not rock, but the chance for Streisand to let that great voice rip carries the sequence along on a wave of energy. This concert is followed almost immediately by a scene depicting Esther recording the Streisand-composed love theme "Evergreen." It's a sweet, simple melody somewhat evocative of "The Way We Were," nicely matched with Paul Williams's lyrics extolling "Love—soft as an easy chair—Love—fresh as the morning air," and every middle-of-the-road cell in the audience's collective body responds to this declaration of love, responding more fully to this melody and lyric than to any of the endless dialogue that precedes and follows it. As the camera lovingly tracks Streisand in a circular pan as she sings, she is the soul of movie stardom—a singular reason for attending an otherwise misshapen, leaden film.

Oddly enough, or maybe not so oddly, the film proved to be an enormous box office success, with both the film and soundtrack reaching #1 on the charts. Perhaps it was not so surprising because the extreme critical bashing Streisand received actually reinforced her audience's connection with her, as it would time and again throughout her career. The critics saw a terrible film, but in Barbra audiences saw a woman mocked and misunderstood, a woman standing up for her own rights and daring to crash through the barriers in her way. These underdog interpretations, which only served to underline the Cinderella aspects of the Streisand career present since it began, were exactly the elements with which the audience identified. Throw in a hit song, additional musical numbers sung by the world's most popular female vocalist, and a doomed romance set in the glittering world of show business, and audiences forgave all, even when the critics forgave nothing. The situation was probably best summed up by a Hollywood insider during pre-production: "It would be nice if the picture was good, but the bottom line is to get her to the studio. Shoot her singing six numbers and we'll make sixty million." End result: They got her to the studio, she sang six numbers, and the movie grossed a great deal more than $60 million.

Swamped with awards from the then notoriously easy Golden Globe voters, *A Star Is Born* was ignored in all major categories by the Academy Awards except for Best Song. At the Oscar ceremony, singing her own composition live on television, a visibly nervous Streisand was introduced by presenter Jane Fonda: "Singing 'Evergreen,' nominated from *A Star Is Born,* is its composer, its star, its executive producer—right on!—Barbra Streisand." Following a huge ovation for the song's performance, Neil Diamond presented the Academy Award for best song to its composer, thereby providing Streisand with a rather nice salve for the wounds incurred by critical slings and arrows.

Streisand had put her reputation on the line, personally and professionally—gambled it all on one throw of the dice—and won. Sort of. She had won in terms of her audience, even expanded her fan base to those who no longer saw her as totally old-fashioned. What she had lost, however, was any critical consideration of her as a serious artist. She could say she didn't care, that the audience was the true judge, but she did care. It would take her many years to gain back that lost ground.

After the intensive labor on *A Star Is Born,* Streisand seemed to enter a new phase of her career: prolonged bouts of inactivity. Although she had always spoken of a lazy side to her personality, her constant flow of multi-media projects had belied that claim. All of that seemed to change, however, in the late 1970s. With Jon Peters firmly in charge of her professional life (longtime personal manager Martin Erlichman was now absent until a 1985 reunion on "The Broadway Album"), Streisand focused on her personal life, releasing collections of greatest hits albums and not filming another movie until 1978's *The Main Event.* Unfortunately, *The Main Event* wasn't worth the wait. The movie was bad, and what is worse, meaningless.

The Main Event reunited Streisand with her *What's Up, Doc?* co-star Ryan O'Neal, in a flat-footed attempt at a zany comedy about mismatched lovers; after a crooked accountant steals all of her money, perfume magnate Hillary Kramer (Streisand) ends up managing washed-up boxer Eddie "Kid Natural" Scanlon (O'Neal), whose contract she unknowingly owns. Forced humor and multiple lingering shots of Streisand's well-toned rear end and legs proved to be the order of the day—not a great recipe for genuine laughs. Streisand's statements that Peters treated her like a person, not a famous thing, and that he thought she had a "great ass," seemed to literally influence the composition of the film. No fewer than four scenes in the film featured extensive footage of the Streisand derriere, and the first of these, taking place in an aerobics class, occupies the entire opening title sequence of the film. Hand in hand with the lingering butt shots are the gatherings of men who wolf whistle at Hillary as she alights from her car. This is all pointless—audiences wouldn't have made Streisand the #1 female box office star in the world if they didn't find her attractive—but in her determination to appear sexy and young, she tries to browbeat the audience into submission.

In addition, the film fails visually; Streisand's Hillary Kramer has earned a great deal of money as an extraordinarily successful businesswoman, yet she lives in an extremely unattractive purple and pink apartment, an apartment so ugly that the viewer wonders if it's all an inside joke by the filmmakers. One almost hopes so, because it just doesn't make sense otherwise, nor do the succession of ridiculous hats Barbra sports throughout the film. In fact it's not just the hats—the clothes themselves aren't any better. Green satin short shorts on a business tycoon?

Barbra's actual performance isn't much better than the film's visual palette. Streisand's Hillary talks so fast that she appears to be trying to break the sound barrier, and her arms flail about from start to finish. This is always a bad sign in a Barbra Streisand movie, because at the most basic level, the arms flap when she is offering no more than a surface interpretation of the character and running roughshod over the material. It is careless acting and even more disappointing after the genuinely comic turns in *The Owl and the Pussycat* and *What's Up, Doc?* It's not an exaggeration to say that the only real laughs in *The Main Event* are generated by O'Neal's fiancée (Patti D'Arbanville) and her hacking smoker's cough.

Ryan O'Neal doesn't fare much better and is saddled with the brunt of the leaden *Star is Born*–type comments on gender roles so beloved by Barbra at this time. To wit: Hillary owns Eddie's contract, and as her employee, he complains that he feels like a piece of meat. Whines O'Neal to Streisand, "You make me feel cheap—used—you don't even tell me how you feel." This Hillary Kramer is as tough and uninteresting as Esther Hoffman Howard in *A Star Is Born,* and ironically these two supposedly sympathetic characters are far more steely than the prostitutes Streisand portrays in *The Owl and the Pussycat* and *Nuts.*

After a series of absurdities which undermine any interest in the plot ("Kid Natural" appears on a talk show with his opponent the day before the fight, and then has first-time sex with manager Streisand that same night, right before the big bout), the film ends with the ultimate absurdity: Hillary throws in the towel, just as Kid Natural is winning the fight, so that they can stay together. This isn't cute—it's stupid. The film ends and over the credits Streisand sings the disposable disco song "The Main Event"—a vocal which has more energy than does the entire film.

Such was Streisand's popularity that the film, aided by the #1 single title tune, proved a box office winner. Fans, however, were beginning to experience a sense of frustration over wasted opportunities which lingers to this day. Even worse, critics had become summarily dismissive.

Why harp on the extreme shortcomings of *A Star Is Born* and *The Main Event*? The answer is that as producer, Streisand had the ultimate say on both films. These were First Artists Ltd. films, and having fought so long and hard for this well-earned power, Barbra wasted it on awful films.

In a way, Streisand, like all artists who become genuine icons (Sinatra, Elvis Presley) had become a victim of her own success. In the workplace she had positioned herself as the leading box office and recording attraction in the world, fulfilling her childhood dreams. Offscreen, she managed to retain a genuine air of mystery, even in the let-it-all-hang-out 1970s. Her reclusiveness and inaccessibility thereby reinforced public interest in her every move. She was called "America's only genuine female superstar"—a term she professed to hate—but this overwhelming success proved a true doubled-edged sword. Every production—and her movies and albums were indeed full-blown Technicolor productions—became an event, a special occasion weighted down with overwhelming expectations. Not only did lightweight trifles such as *The Main Event* sink under such heavy expectations, but the demand to continually repeat the box office success that such lightweight fare generated necessarily limited any sense of artistic growth.

> *She has become an establishment figure, which she certainly wasn't*
> *in the beginning. Of course, time does that to every rebel.*
> —Herb Ross, director/choreographer

Having sworn off theater and concerts due to stage fright, Streisand's only outlets were film and records, media where she could indulge her perfectionist instincts in a totally protected environment. As a result, the press began a new campaign of criticism, harping on Streisand's larger-than-life iconic diva presence. Seemingly in response to such criticism, Streisand, for the first time in her film career, took on a virtually supporting role, in *All Night Long*. The result was the strangest movie of her career, and exhibit #3 in the category of "Oy vey, what was she thinking?"

Streisand undertook the role of Cheryl Gibbons not only as a seeming rebuff to those who criticized her overwhelming front-and-center-in-every-scene screen presence, but also as a favor to her then agent Sue Mengers. Mengers' husband, Jean-Claude Tramont, had begun filming *All Night Long* with Gene Hackman and Australian-born actress Lisa Eichhorn. When problems ensued with Eichhorn's performance, Mengers prevailed upon Streisand to take over the role. It was a disastrous decision in terms of Streisand's career, and proved to be one of the reasons why Streisand and Mengers parted ways.

In *All Night Long,* Barbra's Cheryl Gibbons is a vulnerable suburban blonde sexpot, albeit a low-key one. Married to a boorish fireman (Kevin Dobson), Cheryl is having an affair with her teenaged third cousin Fred Dupler (Dennis Quaid)—or as Fred's father George (Gene Hackman) says to him: "You're having an affair with your mother's sister's late husband's brother's wife." Cheryl proceeds to then fall in love with George, a white-collar executive who is demoted to manager of an all-night drugstore.

Cheryl's greatest ambition is to write country western and Hawaiian songs on the electric organ—not exactly a scenario to set hearts soaring or box office cash registers ringing. Taking all of the previous criticism to heart, Streisand underplays throughout, eschewing any of her familiar mannerisms. Speaking in a soft, breathy voice, adopting a Marilyn Monroe–like wiggle in her walk, her acting is understated, her byplay with Gene Hackman as believable as possible given W.D. Richter's flabby script, there is no grandstanding—and no one cared. Maybe an argument could be made that it's the kiss of death when Barbra's character rides around town on a motorbike, given the fact that the two films wherein she does so are the equally third-rate *For Pete's Sake* and *All Night Long* . . . Whatever the reason, there is exactly one brief funny sequence in the entire film, a clever parody of the "Ride of the Valkyries" sequence in *Apocalypse Now,* complete with toy helicopter. The fun ends there, however, and *All Night Long* registers as soporific and pointless, rather than as a thoughtful, low-key comedy/drama. Not only did no one know quite what to make of a film that is essentially a subdued, off-kilter look at the workplace, American values, and midlife crises, but *All Night Long* presented a Barbra that her fans emphatically did not want to see. Streisand had responded to the critics harping and delivered an effective performance, but the resulting box office gross barely covered her then record $4,000,000 (and 15% of the profit) salary. Damned if she do and damned if she don't.

Upset with this rather large stumble in her career path, Streisand refocused all of her energies and formidable passion on the film property she had obsessively championed since 1968: Isaac Bashevis Singer's "Yentl, the Yeshiva Boy." For the first time in history, a woman would write, produce, direct, and star in a major Hollywood film. And oh yes, sing twelve solo songs. While *All Night Long* had come and gone with barely a ripple on the pond, *Yentl* garnered a flood of press beginning the day the project was officially announced. Hollywood—and Streisand fans—anticipated the film almost as much as did the press. Accusations of megalomania on *A Star Is Born*? Mere bagatelles compared to the press coverage of *Yentl*. Now she thought she could direct? Who did she think she was?

Answer: a very good director. Faced with constant pressure from the studio to stay within budget, and wearing four hats as screenwriter, actress, producer, and director, Streisand faced a barrage of press criticism for overstepping the unwritten yet highly visible boundaries facing women in Hollywood in 1982. Twenty-four years later, with female directors much more common, it is easy to forget what new ground Streisand broke. It wasn't just that a woman was directing a multi-million-dollar picture. It was that one of the biggest names in all of show business was insisting to Hollywood that she and therefore other women were not only capable of directing, but in fact *would* direct. Just as she had in other areas of her career, Streisand demanded a place at the table, and then proceeded to supervise all of the décor, food preparation, and dinner table conversation.

So how is Barbra Streisand's debut as a director on Yentl—*in which she also stars, as well as functioning as co-writer and co-producer? It's a happy occasion. . . . After* Yentl, *it would be rash indeed to sell any of Barbra Streisand's dreams short.*
—Jack Kroll, *Newsweek,* November 28, 1983

Fifteen years in gestation, when *Yentl* finally opened, press reaction seemed divided into two camps: The first expressed admiration for the film, with an undertone of incredulity—"who knew she could do this." The second sought to deny the pleasures the film had given them, dismissing it with a "Yes it was okay, but what megalomania—she didn't let anyone else sing—what was with that designer yarmulke . . ."

Certainly the most personal work Streisand has undertaken in her entire career, *Yentl* represented Barbra's biggest, most public, yet surprisingly intimate, attempt to deal with the loss of her father. If growing up without a father, coupled with her mother's perceived lack of support, were the spurs to a lifetime of relentless ambition and achievement, then *Yentl* represented Streisand's attempt to come to terms with that loss through her art. In effect, *Yentl* is her recreation of her father: a father who loves his daughter and supports her in her quest for knowledge and achievement, no matter how untraditional. The death of Yentl's father spurs her onto her path towards self-fulfillment, albeit disguised as a man, just as Streisand made a career of breaking down what were literally man-made barriers facing women in the entertainment industry. Streisand gives new life to a father in *Yentl,* and then literally and symbolically bids him farewell upon his death. The film is dedicated "To my father—for all our fathers."

What is remarkable is that the film resonated so clearly with audiences across America and throughout the world. After all, in a world of "cop with buddy" pics, a musical film about a Jewish girl who disguises herself as a boy, falls in love with a boy, but marries a beautiful

Jewish girl, set in nineteenth-century Europe no less, did not scream box office potential.

There are two reasons for the success of the film, however:

1. With Streisand's uncanny ability to make her personal issues universal—lack of a father, nonsupportive mother—audiences identified strongly with Yentl's quest for acceptance and freedom. Streisand's outsider status in Hollywood as an ambitious woman in 1983 connected with her graying audience just as it did in 1963, albeit for different reasons.
2. It connected with audiences because it is a very good film, and while *A Star Is Born* has not aged well, *Yentl* holds up in fine fashion.

For starters, the musical soliloquys may have been added in order to ensure financing for the film, but they work very well in the context of the film, supplying a voice for Yentl's strongest desires and yearnings, desires she never would have been able to publicly express in male-dominated nineteenth-century Europe. Written in the form of the questions that Yentl continually asks—"Where Is It Written?," "Papa, Can You Hear Me?," "Will Someone Ever Look at Me That Way?"—the songs provide an underpinning to the quest of the main character.

In addition, when staging the musical sequences, Streisand the director moves seamlessly between singing as interior monologue and moments when Yentl is literally singing onscreen. She establishes this duality in the very first song, "Where Is It Written?," thereby cannily assuring that the musical vocabulary of the piece will be accepted by the audience. In the post-*Cabaret* (1972) world of movie musicals, one wherein audiences demanded a logical reason for each song, this represented an enormous and important directorial achievement.

Physically, the film is quite beautiful, containing picture-postcard images appropriate to the musical fantasy nature of the film. The film is shot in long continuous takes, the camera moving in graceful arcs seemingly synchronized with the arching Michel Legrand melodies and the yearning nature of Yentl herself.

Streisand's obsessive attention to detail pays off handsomely, the film's color scheme of browns and golds adding a rich visual palette. Yentl's journey towards self-

RE-CREATING HER FATHER ON FILM;
DIRECTORIAL DEBUT ON *YENTL*, 1983. *PHOTOFEST*

awareness is mirrored by the recurrent use of water as a symbol of both barrier and renewal throughout the film. The viewer first sees a tiny stream of water in Yentl's village, which is crossed by foot; the body of water becomes a pond crossed by barge, which is succeeded by a swimming hole where Yentl shyly—but not too shyly—peeks at her beloved Avigdor swimming naked, finally culminating in a boat trip across the Atlantic Ocean to the promised land of America.

In addition, there really is not a weak performance in the film, and it's not just the first-rate performances that director Streisand elicits from Amy Irving as Hadass, Yentl's "bride" (Oscar nomination) and from Mandy Patinkin as Avigdor, Yentl's study partner and love interest. It's that Streisand herself gives a terrific performance in her best work since *The Way We Were* nine years earlier. She makes a funny, touching young "boy," no small feat for a then forty-one-year-old woman. She's relaxed onscreen, as if the necessary attention to producing, writing, and directing freed her as an actress, and she has not matched this ease of performance since. She conveys all of the feistiness, complexity, and vulnerability of both Yentl and male alter ego Anshel, and if she justifiably has been criticized for her self-directed wooden performance in *The Prince of Tides,* she did not receive enough credit for her excellent work in *Yentl.*

Yentl is certainly not a perfect film. Eager to make her point about the limited roles allowed to women in the world, Streisand heavy-handedly sets the stage with a traveling bookseller crying out, "Story books for women—sacred books for men" no less than nine times before Yentl even speaks to him. Reinforcing the point repeatedly, she does not allow the audience to discover the situation through images and spare dialogue. With the opening sequences out of the way, however, Streisand the director grows ever more confident, and the film unfolds at a well-paced tempo, neither hurrying nor dawdling, but telling the story in emotional richness without sacrificing detail. In fact, Streisand stumbles for only the second time in the final musical sequence which ends the film.

"A Piece of Sky," the song in which Yentl sings of her desire for "Wanting more—why fly when you can soar?" is a thrilling, all-stops-out theatrical belter which Barbra has used to great effect in her concerts. It makes sense lyrically in the context of the film, but unfortunately Streisand the director has staged the number as a direct echo of the "Don't Rain on My Parade" sequence in *Funny Girl.* The sequence also violates the musical fabric of the entire film leading up to this point. Yes, Yentl is experiencing true freedom on her way to America, and is now feeling free to express her thoughts, but exciting as it is musically, the song is an in-your-face musical showstopper instead of a nuanced examination of character; the viewer is jolted out of the fantasy world so successfully spun until this point. It is the first

time in the film that the viewer thinks, "Hey, how come all those people on the boat aren't looking at this woman running around belting
out a show tune?"

Certainly artistically successful when viewed as an entire film, *Yentl*
remains Streisand's most complete re-working of the central theme
which has informed so much of her life and career and in the process
connected her closely to her core audiences: "Follow your dreams and
appreciate yourself, even if no one else does. If you truly care about
yourself, then don't settle. Ever."

Yentl opened to generally strong reviews, performed solidly at the
box office, and won Streisand a Golden Globe Award for Best Director. Streisand may have been snubbed by the Academy Awards (although Amy Irving was nominated for her supporting performance
and the Legrand/Bergmans score won), but her roll of the dice had
paid off again, even gaining back some of the critical approbation
which had vanished in the morass of *A Star Is Born*. Triumphant but
exhausted, Streisand would not star in another movie for four years.

Occupying herself with her extraordinarily successful *Broadway Album* (1985) and her first public concert in years, albeit one given to an
invited audience at her own Malibu house ("One Voice," 1986), it
wasn't until 1987 that Streisand starred in and produced another motion picture, *Nuts*. Based on Tom Topor's Broadway play of the same
name, *Nuts* chronicles the story of high-priced call girl Claudia
Draper, who murders a client in self-defense. Battling to prove herself
sane and therefore able to stand trial, Draper and her attorney
(Richard Dreyfuss) negotiate the landmines of her past and the scars
resulting from an abusive stepfather (Karl Malden) and a mother
(Maureen Stapleton) who remained silent even while knowing that
the abuse was taking place. Clearly presenting Streisand with rich acting opportunities and carrying some echoes of Streisand's own childhood (one that was not abusive but did contain a disapproving
stepfather [Louis Kind] and a distant mother), *Nuts* was another at-

tempt for Barbra, like so many of the slightly younger baby boomers in her audience, to examine her own childhood, albeit in her case with a $21,000,000 budget and worldwide distribution.

Narcissistic it may have been, but it proved a serious attempt on Streisand's part to examine the powerlessness that so many women feel, the victimization and sexual roles imposed upon them. Concentrating on producing and acting, Streisand left the directing to veteran Martin Ritt (*Hud, Sounder, Norma Rae*). It has been said that Streisand and Ritt clashed repeatedly throughout the filming. On the one hand he thought her too old for the role and found her barrage of opinions and obsessive attention to detail to be excessive and irritating. On the other hand, as producer she was his boss. In the end, they co-existed with a mutual, if wary, respect for each other, and as Ritt assembled a rough cut of the film, he felt that Streisand had turned in a genuinely moving, in-depth performance of nuance and pathos, one which would elicit strong praise for her.

Turning his rough cut over to Streisand the producer, Ritt did not have final control over the re-editing, which Streisand oversaw in full detail. Ritt felt that Streisand beefed up her own already central role at the expense of Maureen Stapleton's moving portrayal of a mother who knows what is happening to her daughter but is too scared to rock the boat. In Ritt's view, the very shape of the film was altered as a result.

Yes, Barbra as Claudia does shout too much, and her climactic speech about refusing to play the parts everyone wants her to play— refusing to be "nuts" for them—simply goes on too long. These are, however, mistakes of editing, not acting, mistakes brought about by the overwhelming desire to be treated with respect as a serious actress. The unfortunate end result is that the film feels too long and somewhat wears out its welcome.

More's the pity, because for all of its star fine-tuning, Streisand's performance proved one of the more moving of her career and for once her complaints about the critics, after the film opened in November '87 to mixed reviews, appeared justified. So powerful was Streisand's star persona in the minds of the press that they could not see past their preconceived ideas of Barbra-the-egomaniacal-star-trying-to-prove-she's-a-serious-actress. They simply undercut any praise they had for her performance with bitchy asides about "Playing a prostitute with a $150 blond highlight job and impeccable backlighting." Yes, the excessive focus on Streisand unbalances the story and shortchanges the subtext of the parental interaction, but the film holds together, and Streisand keeps the famous mannerisms to a minimum. By turns angry, defensive, sarcastic ("You know what I use this dress for? For the ones who want to sit on Mommy's lap."), and believably frightened, Streisand delivers the goods. She quite admirably conveys the vulnerability beneath Claudia Draper's tough exterior, no easy task given how unlikeable the character is in many ways.

With mixed-to-negative reviews, however, and a downbeat story far removed from more typical Streisand fare, crowds were not enthusiastic, business was mediocre at best, and Streisand's dream of another Academy Award for acting was dashed by the lack of even a nomination. Bruised but unbowed, she once again decided to put her reputation, stature, and power on the line with a film she felt it was her destiny to make. She would star in, produce, and direct a feature film based upon Pat Conroy's best seller *The Prince of Tides*.

What attracted Streisand to *The Prince of Tides* were the twin elements that attracted her to any project about which she felt passionate: one, a central character with whom she identified and who provided her with a rich multilayered acting opportunity, and two, issues of childhood neglect and the feelings of being an outsider coupled with an examination of the role of women in today's society.

The Prince of Tides concerns the suicidal poet Savannah Wingo (Melinda Dillon), her brother Tom (Nick Nolte) and mother Lila

(Kate Nelligan), and the New York psychiatrist Susan Lowenstein (Streisand) who attempts to treat Savannah by unlocking the secrets of her South Carolina childhood and family. A childhood marred by abuse, an emotionally distant mother, and a successful, strong New York Jewish woman who falls in love with the WASPy Tom Wingo—this was material to which Streisand could relate.

The Prince of Tides actually forms a neat bookend with *Yentl*, because if *Yentl* concerns itself with father-daughter interaction, *The Prince of Tides* delves into mother-child relationships. Tom's relationship with his mother Lila informs his entire life, past and present, and Lowenstein deals not only with that family history, but also with her own troubled relationship with son Bernard (adding another layer to the film was the fact that Streisand's own son, Jason Gould, played Bernard). It is a movie about forgiveness, and if close friend and colleague Marilyn Bergman found it to be about Barbra "forgiving her own mother," Barbra herself placed the film in the even larger context of acceptance: "When I was faced with the potential loss of my mother [due to heart problems], the movie became much easier . . . It took the proper place—it's much more secondary to life. That's what *The Prince of Tides* is about—in a way—learning to accept your mother." In short, it was another attempt to deal with her own childhood, sort out her past, and examine how past mistreatment informed her present-day adulthood. Streisand felt certain there would be an audience for this universal material, and filming began in the spring of 1990.

By the time filming and editing were completed, the advance buzz on *The Prince of Tides* was very strong, and the late-1991 release of the film provided Streisand with the critical and popular success she craved—albeit with one rather large caveat. Streisand the director was almost universally praised, Streisand the actress universally criticized.

By nearly any standard, *The Prince of Tides* is an extremely accomplished and effective piece of filmmaking. This was not ego run

amok, but rather a mature artist telling a rich emotional story. Beautifully shot (by cinematographer Stephen Goldblatt) and instantly conveying the languid beauty of the South Carolina coast, the film
effortlessly shuttles between past and present, between sequences of
Tom and Savannah's childhood on the water, and the nightmarish
present-day legacy of that childhood which has led Savannah to attempt suicide.

So skilled is the storytelling that in the first five minutes of the
film, the viewer learns about the troubled relationship between Tom
and Savannah's parents, the importance of the beautiful, brooding
landscape in all of their lives, and the difficult childhood all three
Wingo children tried to endure. This past/present juxtaposition is a
big reason why the film resonates; the viewer is made fully aware of
the Wingos trying and failing to outrun their pasts. In conveying this
dichotomy, Streisand strikes nary a false note. There is a beautiful tran-
sition from Tom's life as a child ("before I decided to have no
money") to scenes of Tom as an adult with his own children. A second
seamless cut takes Nolte from a late-night run on the South Carolina
beach directly into his new life in New York City, and as the camera
travels from the Manhattan skyline to the noise and traffic of New
York City streetlife, one realizes that an assured and gifted director is at
the helm.

The storytelling is surehanded and in fact the only set piece in the
film which doesn't work occurs towards the end when Lowenstein
and Tom, having now fallen in love, spend the weekend at her country
"cabin." This sequence plays like a Ralph Lauren Polo ad come to life,
and Lowenstein and Tom all but run to each other in slow motion.
This hiccup aside, Streisand elicits believable performances from not
only the children portraying the Wingos as youngsters, but also from
Dillon as the troubled Savannah, and especially Nelligan as willful ma-
triarch Lila. Jason Gould turns in a well-grounded, nuanced portrayal
as Lowenstein's resentful son Bernard, and what could have been

DIRECTING *THE PRINCE OF TIDES,* 1991. DIRECTORS GUILD OF AMERICA NOMINATION, BUT NO OSCAR RECOGNITION. *PHOTOFEST*

jeered at as nepotism instead proves praiseworthy. Dominating the proceedings is Nolte, giving the best performance of his career as the macho yet sensitive football coach Tom Wingo. Streisand elicits a performance from the talented Nolte which hits every note in portraying the decent, honorable husband and father still haunted by his childhood, a man vulnerable to the attractions of a woman not his wife, yet committed to the honorable course of action. Watching the shift of expressions on Nolte's face as he studies Bernard playing the violin—the change from pride to envy and finally to awe—is to see great acting define character without one word being spoken. Terrific performances all around, but there is one problem that keeps the film from being a truly great one—Streisand's own central performance as Dr. Lowenstein.

Directing herself as the scared, brave, burgeoning young woman Yentl, she had turned in a moving, complex performance. It may very well be that playing a girl masquerading as a boy in nineteenth-century Europe freed Streisand from concerns of modern-day beauty, but portraying the intelligent, intuitive, yet vulnerable Lowenstein, she looks great but is stiff and almost ungainly. Perhaps it was the focus on all other aspects of the production which clouded her vision, but the old obsessions about appearance and beauty resurface here to the detriment of the film. Lowenstein oftentimes appears in filtered golden light, carefully backlit—the eye cannot focus anywhere else but on Lowenstein. This is a psychiatrist on whom the focus always remains, even while she is in session with a patient. When Tom Wingo finally confronts his nightmarish past, breaking down in sobs as he recalls childhood horrors, he buries his head on Lowenstein's shoulder; the problem is that the ensuing close-up is then of Lowenstein's face and tears, not Tom's. The breakthrough is the patient's, not the doctor's, but the viewer wouldn't know it.

Most damning of all, one is aware of Streisand giving a "performance" as a serious intellectual, knitting her brows to convey grave concern over her patient. Gone is the sense of spontaneity and quick intelligence that informed her best work, as in *The Way We Were*. Katie Morosky would have had no use for the stolid Lowenstein. While the performance is not nearly as bad as the film's detractors would have it, interestingly enough, it is only in Lowenstein's scenes with her son Bernard that Streisand, playing opposite her own son, Jason, relaxes. Here the different facets of her character finally appear; the loving yet somewhat troubled and demanding relationship between mother and son unleashes the instinctual actress in Streisand and the character comes to life.

Streisand's performance aside, the film proved popular with both critics and audiences, and garnered seven Academy Award nominations, including Best Picture (for which Streisand would have won an Oscar as Producer), Best Actor (Nolte) and Best Supporting Actress (Nelligan). Although nominated for the prestigious Directors Guild Award as

Best Director, Streisand was snubbed by the Academy, an omission that garnered somewhat more press attention than that accorded the five nominees: Jonathan Demme (winner for *The Silence of the Lambs*), Oliver Stone (*JFK*), Barry Levinson (*Bugsy*), John Singleton (*Boyz n the Hood*), and Ridley Scott (*Thelma and Louise*). Judging by statements she made, Streisand was stung by the omission, and by the criticism of her own performance, but took quiet satisfaction in the fact that even so she was now acknowleged as a serious, talented director by critics and public alike. She had now regained almost all of the artistic ground she had lost fifteen years earlier with *A Star Is Born* and *The Main Event*. What would consolidate this standing, and solidify her artistic reputation, would be the all important follow-up film to *The Prince of Tides*. The perfect subject matter appeared to be at hand with Streisand's renewed attempts to film Larry Kramer's incendiary AIDS drama *The Normal Heart*. With another strong female role at its core—at least as Streisand shaped the screenplay—*The Normal Heart* explored the beginnings of the key worldwide health issue of the second half of the twentieth century—the AIDS epidemic. Hopes were high for the film—and then . . .

And then the ten-year (!) process of shaping the piece with Kramer, of obtaining and renewing rights, fell apart. Rights had first been acquired in 1986 and with typical Streisand immersion, work on multiple drafts of the script with Kramer had continued until collapsing over the issue of control and final credit. Renegotiating for the rights in 1990, work was again delayed by the years of effort Streisand expended on *The Prince of Tides*. Work began a third time, but Streisand, determined to make a film that proved her to be a commercially successful director, chose to make *The Mirror Has Two Faces* instead. Preoccupied with work on *Mirror*, she allowed her option on the material to lapse, and when Kramer publicly attacked her for prolonging the process while he battled AIDS himself, the hopes for the film came to a screeching halt.

More's the pity, because instead of taking risks on a highly political film dealing with an international plague, Streisand chose to make a glossy film dealing with the issue eternally close to her heart: plain woman, misunderstood by her controlling mother, really is beautiful—inside and out—finds herself, and in the process finds her true love, who just happens to be hunky and WASPy. Fade out.

Fully confident in the finished product, Streisand was apparently shocked by the hostile critical tone and indifferent box office response to *The Mirror Has Two Faces*. She shouldn't have been, for two simple reasons:

1. The public had long ago accepted her as a unique beauty—not just beautiful because of her talent, but also because of her trim, increasingly glamorous appearance. As a result, the public had long since moved on, and Streisand was in effect re-working familiar territory about which only she cared.
2. *The Mirror Has Two Faces* is not a very good film.

For starters, *The Mirror Has Two Faces* contains enough plot to stock any three soap operas. Ugly duckling college professor Rose Morgan (Streisand), overshadowed by her beautiful sister (Mimi Rogers) and mother (Lauren Bacall), enters into a celibate marriage of friendship with handsome fellow professor Gregory Larkin (Jeff Bridges). When Rose's feelings toward Gregory turn romantic, he rejects her and flees. Rose embarks on a fitness and makeover program, and when Gregory returns he is wowed by the newly blonde and streamlined Rose, as is (soon-to-be-ex) brother-in-law, Alex (Pierce Brosnan). In the end, Rose triumphantly reunites with Gregory, but on her own terms.

The first half of the film is actually quite likeable and amiable and begins promisingly enough with a first shot of wallflower Rose wearing a cold-cream mask and eating a cupcake. When she does go on her first date with Gregory, a dinner at an expensive restaurant, she wears a turtleneck to dinner. This girl clearly needs help. A similar sense of fun pervades an amusing vignette wherein Jeff Bridges calls a phone-sex service and the femme fatale on the line turns out to be a dowdy middle-aged woman sitting in her kitchen while she breathily promises sexual favors. Best of all, there is a first-rate performance from Lauren Bacall as Streisand's mother, detonating wisecracks in her seen-it-all baritone: Frustrated by her daughter Rose, Bacall barks: "I never should have encouraged you to speak."

It had been so long since the ultra-serious Streisand allowed herself to be funny onscreen (her last comedy being 1979's *The Main Event*) that it is actually a kick to see her in funny-girl mode; whether battling with her crooked hairpiece or begging off an unwelcome date so that she can stay home and watch the Yankees game, there is a lightness about her performance which has been missing for years—funny girl indeed. But not for long.

As soon as husband Gregory has rejected Rose and left, all the light disappears from the movie while Rose wills herself to thinness and glamour. The film loses all sense of pacing and the rather fun first half is displaced by a ponderous essay on women and the concept of beauty. The new Rose is absolutely no fun and before long, yep—blond highlights, cleavage, and backlighting rear their customary heads. Rose/Streisand is now able to reject not just one but two handsome WASP princes.

Most damaging of all, it seemingly never occurred to Streisand that many viewers at the end of the twentieth century would simply not accept the central conceit of a deliberately celibate marriage between the two heterosexual leading characters. Without the acceptance of this conceit, what should be a winning romantic comedy with serious overtones quickly turns into an uphill slog.

This literally unbelievable premise makes the whole film seem leaden, because each complication along the way (and romantic come-

dies onscreen are all about complications) just delays not only the inevitable but also the obvious. Of course Rose and Gregory both want
sex and will have it—they're fifty years old and they are human be-
ings. Supporting player George Segal's remark to his friend Gregory
unfortunately sums it all up: "You're a very sick man, you know that."

Yes, there are positive aspects to the film. Certainly, many of the
themes Streisand explores in *Mirror* are valid: concepts of beauty, female competition, mother-daughter conflicts, and the idea of an older
woman (Bacall) still feeling young inside. The film is beautifully shot
and lit, with a nice production design by Tom John. There are even
moments when the Streisand magic shines through; when Gregory rejects Rose's physical advances by bluntly telling her, "I took every precaution to make sure there was no physical attraction," the viewer
feels Rose's vulnerability. Streisand, fifty-four years old at the time of
filming, could still produce a feeling in the viewer that she needs to be
protected. The problem is that the nice-looking production and exploration of valid issues are offset by the fact that the issues are rarely
framed properly.

For starters, there are some unintentional howlers along the way,
with college classroom scenes more unrealistic than those seen in any
movie since, well, *On a Clear Day*. Streisand's Professor Rose Morgan
is presented as such a spellbinder in the classroom that students not
only fill the vast lecture hall, but stand on the stairs just to hear her
pearls of wisdom. In what would seem a clear example of no one being able to say no to star/producer/director/songwriter Streisand, she
actually left a scene in the final cut in which a student gets so caught
up in what Professor Morgan states in class, that he grins and raises his
fist in a "right on" salute left over from 1968. The mind boggles.

Most damaging of all, the final thirty minutes of the movie,
wherein Rose triumphs, lie absolutely inert because director Streisand
doesn't trust her audience and pounds home her themes over and over
again. When the newly glamorized Rose dumps Gregory, he is pre-

sented as being so distraught that he slumps over and literally falls to the ground. Both Pierce Brosnan and Jeff Bridges are saddled with endless dialogue wherein they explain why they now love the beautiful, sexy, smart Rose. Jeff Bridges's Gregory is shown to be so smitten with Rose by the end of the film that he grapples with her doorman in a desperate attempt to gain entrance to her building. At this point, just in case the viewer hasn't caught on, the following dialogue is belted home:

> **Rose:** What did you want to say?
> **Gregory:** God, you're beautiful.

The ugly duckling motif which has now run through *Funny Girl, The Owl and the Pussycat, The Way We Were,* and *Funny Lady,* has reached its ultimate and most unnecessary incarnation. It's unnecessary because while Rose may triumph, by this point no one cares, and it's the ultimate manifestation of this theme because when Gregory says to Rose, "I don't care if you're pretty—I love you anyway," the ugly duckling motif can thankfully go no further.

There is a double frustration at work here; not only should the second half of the film have been much better, but even a somewhat casual viewer is left with disbelief that with all of her extravagant gifts, this trifle is the best Streisand could come up with, the best material she could find to lavish her time, talent, and passion upon. Where indeed is *The Normal Heart*?

Television

The result was a pinacle moment in American show business, in any form, in any period. She is so great it is shocking, something like being in love. . . . She may well be the most supremely talented and complete popular entertainer that this country has ever produced. . . . She touches you to your toes. And then she knocks you out.

—United Press International review of *My Name Is Barbra,* Streisand's first television special, 1965

An embarrassing outing, a concoction of deranged productions that not even the star and her major colleague of the evening, Jason Robards, could straighten out.

—Jack Gould, *The New York Times* on *The Belle of 14th Street,* Streisand's third television special, 1967

Over the years, Streisand has become such a familiar presence, such an accepted part of the establishment in Hollywood, in the music industry, and on the political scene, that it is easy to forget what a startling presence she was on television in the 1960s. Skinny, nasal, dressed in secondhand clothes, intensely dramatic and talking one hundred miles per hour, Barbra Streisand was an apparition—a KOOK. A total anomaly in the days of polite, well-dressed, demure singers, Streisand proved startling—abrasive and shocking even—to the Perry Como television–watching, Doris Day movie–going audience. She was unapologetically Jewish, and in the early 1960s when ethnicity was submerged to a large extent, she was proud of her Jewishness. To every misfit across America, male or female, miserable in his or her attempt to fit in with the prevailing social mores and behavior, she sent a very strong message; most important of all, it was a message that could be received on television in their very living rooms. The message was simple and powerful: You are not alone. And, the audience thought, if she can do it, maybe so can I. Of course, they couldn't do it in such a spectacular fashion, because no one else had that sort of immense talent, but it didn't matter. There was hope. And the intense, almost frightening identification with, and idolatry of, Streisand began.

Barbra's first television appearance was on *The Jack Paar Tonight Show*, with Orson Bean guest hosting. She made a very favorable impression and subsequently appeared on *The Joe Franklin Show* in New York City and the nationwide *Gary Moore Show,* singing her then signature song of "Happy Days Are Here Again." What really introduced American audiences to her, however, were her thirteen appearances on *PM East,* hosted by Mike Wallace. Even in the face of strong studio-executive opposition to this bizarre creature named Barbra Streisand, producer Mert Koplin insisted upon booking Streisand and she became a semi-regular guest. Usually singing a song to strong applause, Streisand would then sit down and launch into a discourse on "crazy" topics like the dangers of drinking milk. These talk segments, combined with her oftentimes outlandish appearance, proved the key to Streisand's "kook" label. It was all calculated by Barbra—even then the director—for maximum impact and she oftentimes suggested a topic for discussion. Launching into a tirade against powerful producer David Susskind for not being open to new talent (in and of itself a dangerous move, especially for an unknown young girl) Streisand herself perfectly captured why she proved so memorable, with the Brooklynese zinger: "I scare you, don't I? I'm so far out, I'm in."

This exchange was monitored by host Mike Wallace. Thirty years later, he hosted the *60 Minutes* segment profiling Streisand at the time of *The Prince of Tides.* The segment provides a fascinating mirror image of their interaction on *PM East* thirty years earlier. This time, interviewer and subject are powerful equals, and when superstar Barbra, in full director mode, asks the television crew to change the lighting, her technical expertise displayed by her request for very specific equipment changes, a visibly annoyed Wallace barks, "Can we just start the interview, please?"

This dialogue is followed minutes later by Wallace bringing up the subject of Streisand's distant, withholding mother, reducing Streisand to tears. Watching Wallace's subsequent interview with Diana Streisand Kind, one appreciates why Barbra has spoken so often of her mother never uttering words of praise (and one gains a better understanding of Streisand's strained relations with stepfather Louis Kind, who unfeelingly told seven-year-old Barbra that she couldn't have ice cream because she was ugly). When asked point-blank by Wallace if she was proud of Barbra, Diana Kind answers the question with a question: "Who wouldn't be proud of such a girl?" Mrs. Kind seems incapable of simply saying "I'm proud of my daughter." It's as if Mrs. Kind, unsure of her own place in the world in 1943 when her husband died, leaving her to raise two young children alone, is still unsure of the world at large and even of her wildly successful daughter's place in it. Any words of praise for Barbra lay three years in the future, reluctantly offered after one of Barbra's brilliant 1994 concerts.

The interview proceeds along its fascinating, bumpy road, as evidenced by the next exchange between Wallace and Streisand:

> **Wallace:** You don't do enough singing. You didn't sing in the film. This disappointed me in *The Prince of Tides*.
> **Streisand:** *(annoyed)* I've made forty-five albums.

Taking Streisand back to see her first-ever apartment in Manhattan, reporter and star exchange barbed comments:

> **Wallace:** Thirty years ago I didn't like you.
> **Streisand:** I thought you were mean . . . Why do you sound so accusatory?

Two control freaks, Wallace in his seventies, Streisand soon to turn fifty, both used to their every wish or command being carried out instantly, verbally slugging it out toe to toe. It is a neat little textbook example of how two very powerful, abrasive personalities can irritate and exasperate, but still fascinate. Indeed, it is almost a scholarly illustration of star power and personality, and why each of these stars matters. Thirty years after their initial meetings, neither gives an inch, and

ONE UNHAPPY STAR—THE CONTENTIOUS INTERVIEW WITH
MIKE WALLACE. *60 MINUTES,* 1991. *PHOTOFEST*

each still displays a naked hunger, the constant need to control events and be the center of attention. With all of the accolades they've each accumulated, it is never enough for either one. It never can be.

Consolidating her growing profile by combining appearances in increasingly upscale nightclubs (the Lion led to the Bon Soir which led to Basin Street East) with television appearances, Barbra Streisand was fully introduced to the majority of Americans with two memorable nationwide television appearances. The first, a guest appearance on *The Ed Sullivan Show* in 1963, gave her the chance to belt out the bluesy, hyper-dramatic Arlen/Mercer standard "When the Sun Comes Out" on a stage floor filled with umbrellas (!). And, following a performance of "Miss Marmelstein" from *I Can Get It For You Wholesale* on *The Bob Hope Show,* there was, most memorably of all, a guest appearance on *The Judy Garland Show.*

Garland's unfortunately short-lived television series was an up-and-down affair, with the high points as good as anything seen on television. Forty years later, two moments immediately come to mind: Garland nearly shouting "The Battle Hymn of the Republic" in tribute to the recently assassinated President John F. Kennedy, and the memorable "Be My Guest" segment with rising newcomer Barbra Streisand.

For her guest appearance on the show, Streisand sang two solos: "Down With Love" and "Bewitched, Bothered and Bewildered," and great as they were, as were Garland's own solos, nothing quite compares to the two icons dueting. First up was a medley of "Hooray for Love/After You've Gone/By Myself/'S Marvelous/How About You/Lover Come Back to Me/You and the Night and the Music/It All Depends on You." Similarly attired in white pants and checked shirts, their voices blending beautifully together, the legend and the legend-in-the-making give a lesson in what star power is all about. The segment also contained some genuinely witty banter:

> **Barbra:** Well, if I really am your guest I have a small request.
> **Judy:** Anything you want to do.
> **Barbra:** Anything?
> **Judy:** Anything.
> **Barbra:** Can I replace you?
> **Judy:** *(wryly)* Be my guest, be my guest.

Which really was the point and why the segment is so terrific, forty years later: Streisand *is* Garland's successor. The same hyper-emotional approach to a song, the wide vibrato employed for emotional effect, the half-concealed sob while singing, the acting out of the lyrics. The neediness. With Garland, it was the need for the audience's love, the reassurance that they would stay with her, no matter what, all the way over the rainbow. With Streisand it was the need to be told she was beautiful, the desperate yearning for a bigger, better world just over the horizon, where all of her Technicolor dreams could be satisfied. And so, when they dueted on their theme titled "Happy" songs—Judy singing "Get Happy" in counterpoint to Barbra's "Happy Days Are Here Again," a perfect match Garland herself discovered one day while singing along to Streisand's recording—it's not just the thrilling sound. It's watching Streisand, a fearless twenty-one-year-old, realize "Hey—I'm singing with the best, and she's magic, and I'm just as good." Streisand has spoken often of Garland grabbing her hand and her surprise that Judy's hand was shaking, the twenty-one-year-old Streisand not understanding why. Decades later, buffeted by her own, albeit very different personal and professional travails, Streisand simply stated, "Now I know why."

To complete this memorable show, there is also a hilarious additional guest appearance by Ethel Merman, who swaggers onto the set and, when all three women begin to sing "There's No Business Like Show Business," completely drowns out both Garland and Streisand, neither one of them exactly shrinking violets in the belting department. It's also funny to watch Streisand's reaction to Merman. At first, Streisand is busy trying, somewhat unsuccessfully, to remember the lyrics to "There's No Business Like Show Business." Then, when the full volume of Merman's belting reaches the decibel level of jet planes taking off, Streisand, a bemused expression on her face, shoots a look which seems to say, "Can you believe this chick? Is she for real?"

The show also provides an interesting example of why Merman never really succeeded on film whereas Garland and Streisand did. In their different ways, Judy and Barbra both traded on a genuine vulnerability that the camera instantly conveyed. One would have to search for the better part of a millennium to discover any vulnerability in Merman. Her rather foursquare approach to both acting and singing tended to run roughshod over the material at hand, and while this approach worked for her when separated from the audience by the proscenium arch of the theater, it is simply too in-your-face for the television or movie screen. Great as Merman was onstage, subtlety was never exactly her strong suit, and like another Broadway musical diva, Carol Channing, she never learned to scale down her performance for the camera.

The successful appearance on the Judy Garland show was followed by Streisand's knock-'em-out, razzle-dazzle triumph in *Funny Girl* on Broadway. It wasn't just a brief magazine article now—it was the cover of

THE HISTORY-MAKING DUETS WITH JUDY GARLAND ON GARLAND'S CBS TELEVISION SERIES, 1963. WHEN MERMAN JOINED IN, STREISAND AND GARLAND WERE RENDERED INAUDIBLE. *PHOTOFEST*

LIFE magazine. Streisand was the hottest star in the business and, in very short order, had her own deal with CBS for five television specials. The first, *My Name Is Barbra,* was filmed and aired during the Broadway run of *Funny Girl.* How, people wondered, would the kook with the big nose look on screen? How would she play in Peoria? The answer: sensationally.

MAGNIFICENT BARBRA

—Caption to front-page picture of Streisand in the *New York Journal American* the morning after *My Name Is Barbra,* Streisand's first television special, aired on CBS

One of the keys to the overwhelming success of *My Name Is Barbra* was longtime manager Martin Erlichman, who insisted that CBS give total artistic control to Streisand. Network variety specials of the day traditionally stuck to the tried-and-true formula of a star, several guests, banter, solo musical turns by the star, and group numbers. Streisand and Erlichman insisted that the entire hour would feature only Barbra—no guest stars, no group numbers, no nothing. In 1965, this was an enormous break with tradition, and in a neat foreshadowing of upcoming battles with recording and film executives throughout the years, Streisand won this battle of wills. The special would be all Barbra all the time. This technique would win her critical brickbats in the future, but for this first special it proved sensational. With talent like this, who wanted anyone else around? As would happen throughout her career, Streisand gambled it all on one throw of the dice—and won. Big time.

What is particularly impressive is how skilled Streisand proved at adapting to the camera. For all of the talk of odd looks, hers was a face made for the camera. The unusual planes of her face dominated by the large nose—it all somehow made sense on camera. Her untraditional looks meant that there was always a new image to present; one could emphasize the nose (left side definitely preferred by Ms. Streisand) or cut away from the nose to the intense, close-set eyes. Boring the visual never was. And, instinctively, Barbra knew to minimize her gestures and facial expressions on camera. She understood that there was no second balcony to reach. What there was was a television audience of tens of millions, and very specifically, Hollywood film executives who doubted her viability on the big screen.

Smartly directed by Dwight Hemion and beautifully designed by Tom John, *My Name Is Barbra* also benefited enormously from the contribution of Joe Layton. A well-known, highly respected Broadway director and choreographer, Layton conceived the musical numbers (a job he repeated on *Color Me Barbra,* which he also coproduced with Dwight Hemion). Working closely with Streisand in shaping the flow of the specials, Layton proved instrumental in helping the shows achieve a seamless, elegant quality, one difficult to ever achieve in musical variety specials and virtually unheard of forty years ago.

My Name Is Barbra, broadcast on April 28, 1965, was neatly divided into three segments. Act I presented Barbra as a five-year-old child playing amidst oversized furniture. Even at this point in her career, Streisand was exploring her past

THE GROUNDBREAKING, AWARD-WINNING FIRST TELEVISION SPECIAL. *MY NAME IS BARBRA,* 1965. *PHOTOFEST*

traumas in her work, albeit in a lighthearted manner. With background shrieks of children yelling "Crazy Barbra, Crazy Barbra," Streisand sang self-defining songs of yearning: "Much More," which could have served as her career and life theme song; "I'm Late," which according to growing press reports she always was; "Make Believe," which her entire life was about; "My Pa," the lifelong void; and her signature song, "People." These songs also, not so coincidentally, displayed Barbra's vulnerability and won doubters over to her side. Calculated and heartfelt at the same time, Streisand here wielded vulnerability as a weapon.

Act II, an extended fashion-show segment set in a deserted

Bergdorf Goodman, presented kooky Barbra, the thrift-shop devotee, in the tony setting of Bergdorf's. Set to all-stops-out orchestrations by Peter Matz, "Give Me the Simple Life" found Barbra in an enormous feathered hat, "I Got Plenty of Nothin'" presented her in a backless dress, and the grand ironic finale to the medley, a beautifully suited Barbra, standing near very expensive-looking jewelry, warbled "The Best Things in Life Are Free."

After the busy second act, which gave full reign to Streisand's wacky and camp sensibility, the third and final segment went back to basics: Barbra in concert, alone in a spotlight, the essence of stardom. Here I Am. Here I'll Stay. Even at twenty-three, there were already enough songs associated with her for this to be a greatest hits concert: "When the Sun Comes Out," "Lover Come Back to Me," "Don't Rain on My Parade," "The Music that Makes Me Dance," "My Man," "Happy Days Are Here Again." One home run after another. Other stars needed? *What* other stars?!

My Name Is Barbra proved a ratings winner and garnered five Emmy Awards, including two top Emmys: Outstanding Program Achievement in Entertainment and Outstanding Individual Achievement by an Actor or Performer. As would happen so often in her career, the process of filming the special proved in one sense painful, every decision obsessed over, driving her fellow workers to distraction. But the end result proved Streisand correct. At least thus far, she really did know better, and CBS wanted another special. Quickly.

Eleven months later, on March 30, 1966, CBS aired *Color Me Barbra* to a second round of critical raves and high audience ratings.

> *It's difficult to see how any other television musical show*
> *can top it for the rest of the year. Unless, of course, a third*
> *Barbra Streisand program is to be scheduled.*
> —Leon Mishkin, *New York Morning Telegraph* on *Color Me Barbra*,
> Streisand's second television special

One of the first television specials filmed in the then unique (for television) color format, *Color Me Barbra* hewed closely to the successful formula originated in *My Name Is Barbra:* The special would be divided into three segments and she would be the only performer.

Act I featured Barbra (often literally) running through the empty Philadelphia Museum of Art (echoes of the empty Bergdorf Goodman—what Barbra wanted, Barbra got), singing songs appropriate to particular paintings. She appeared as the similarly profiled Queen Nefertiti, singing "Where or When" with mounting intensity, and performed "Gotta Move" as a living piece of pop art.

Mood and tone were shifted to the comical as Streisand sang a very witty medley of songs, courtesy of Peter Matz arrangements, to a group of exotic animals in a circus setting: "Sam, You Made the Pants Too Long" was danced and sung to a group of penguins; rubbing noses with an anteater, Barbra proclaimed "We've Got So Much in Common," which led to the poignant little-girl-lost query in song, "Have I Stayed Too Long at the Fair." The segment culminated in a joyful "Look at that Face," sung to Streisand's own poodle, Sadie (a gift from the *Funny Girl* company).

A solo concert concluded the hour, just as it had in *My Name Is Barbra.* This featured a knock-out rendition of "Where Am I Going" from Broadway's *Sweet Charity,* and in typical ironic Streisand fashion, she ended the show with "Starting Here, Starting Now." The latter song in particular (propelled by a first-rate Don Costa arrangement) proved perfectly suited to showing off the primal appeal of Streisand's voice, with lyrics stressing the over-the-rainbow kind of love she yearned for so strongly:

> . . . *Take my hand*
> *For the greatest journey*
> *Heaven can allow*
> *Starting love, starting here, starting now . . .*

NEFERTITI AND PAL: "WHERE OR WHEN." *COLOR ME BARBRA* **TELEVISION SPECIAL, 1966.** *PHOTOFEST*

This is all sung with mounting intensity against an orchestral progression of ascending chords until, just when you think a breaking point has been reached, Streisand, with deliberate emphasis, releases the audience's expectations with a breathy "Now—take my hand." She has pulled the audience along with her on the journey; at the end of the hour there is a sense of beginnings, of that magical word in the Streisand lexicon, *possibilities.*

The result was dazzling. Critics raved, ratings were high, and Emmy nominations ensued (although the show ended up losing the top Emmy awards to Frank Sinatra's *A Man and His Music*). After two triumphant television specials, Streisand appeared that much closer to her lifelong goal—starring in a Hollywood movie. But first, CBS wanted a third special. This time, the formula would be altered—with disastrous results.

For this one special, Barbra would act as "host" for a recreation of turn-of-the-century 14th Street in New York City. There were to be two co-stars, Jason Robards, Jr., and John Bubbles, and a chorus composed of "Lee Allen and the Beef Trust Girls." To view the resulting show today (the show is entitled *The Belle of 14th Street*) is to experience two reactions: embarrassment, and an incredulous reaction of "What was she thinking?"

Typical of the show's mishmash of style and content was a scene from *The Tempest* featuring Jason Robards as Prospero, and Barbra as both Miranda and a flying Ariel. Neither funny nor intriguing—just silly—this skit was, unfortunately, no worse than Streisand performing a very ill-conceived duet with herself in which she played both a German opera singer performing "Liebestraum" and a young boy in the audience singing "Mother Macree." This conceit falls flat enough to cause Mother Macree herself to let loose with a few oy veys. There is a truly embarrassing chorus line of extremely overweight women, "The Beef Trust Girls," an idea that audiences, and feminist Streisand herself, would seemingly never allow to see the light of day today.

There was, however, one redeeming feature of the hour: the solo concert that closed the show. Sporting a picture hat and feather boa, Streisand sang pop classics in a straightforward, no-frills manner that belatedly served to remind the audience of how great a singer she could be. "My Melancholy Baby," "I'm Always Chasing Rainbows," "Some of These Days," and especially a limpid, tender medley of "My Buddy" and "How About Me" that showed her voice at possibly its most beautiful ever—it was the equivalent of vocal honey, or in the immortal words of Linda Richman, "Like buttah."

The closing medley was not enough to salvage the preceding heavy-handed forty minutes, however. Critics were unkind, ratings were low, and Columbia did not release the soundtrack it had prepared. To this day, the soundtrack of the special has never been released, although "My Buddy/How About Me" surfaced on the *The Way We Were* vocal album, serving as very welcome filler on an album hastily released to capitalize on the enormous success of the title song. *The Belle of 14th Street* was a concept gone wrong. Barbra and Martin Erlichman had been right all along: Barbra alone was the best musical special.

A Happening in Central Park, Barbra's solo concert in Central Park for 135,000 fans, was filmed live on June 17, 1967 (four months before the broadcast of *The Belle of 14th Street*), but not broadcast until September 1968. Streisand, who was nervous about security because of the recently concluded Israeli-Arab Six Day War and threats she had received, interrupted work on the film of *Funny Girl* and flew back to New York for the free concert. The timing and logistics of the concert proved remarkable for two reasons:

1. Streisand flew *back* to New York City for the concert. Indelibly associated with New York City, what no one at the time realized was that Streisand was no longer a New Yorker (a fact that added a second layer of irony to the *New York Times* headline review of the 1994 concerts at Madison Square Garden: LOCAL GIRL MAKES GOOD, SINGS). At age twenty-five she had moved to California, seemingly for the rest of her life.

2. The security threats and the staggering size of the crowd, which at one point pushed en masse towards the stage, had an enormous impact on Streisand's already burgeoning stage fright and therefore on her career. This stage fright was increased when she momentarily forgot the words to one of her songs. It would be twenty-seven years before Streisand embarked on a concert tour again—twenty-seven years before she would sing publicly before an arena-sized crowd in

New York. (The decision to stop performing would also impact Streisand's record sales. Yes, she became the best-selling female vocalist in the world, but how much greater would the sales have been if she had toured or granted more than the very occasional interview?)

The Central Park Happening itself? A perfectly pleasant run-through of hits such as "Cry Me a River" and "He Touched Me," balanced with signature songs "People" and the closer "Happy Days Are Here Again." Interspersed throughout were the ditties "Value," from her one-night theatrical run in *Another Evening with Harry Stoones,* and "Marty the Martian." The extreme humidity caused problems with the strings in the orchestra and resulted in some off-key orchestra playing (e.g., the climax of "He Touched Me"), but Streisand was remarkably successful in creating an intimate feeling throughout the evening, no small feat with 135,000 fans gathered in the middle of Central Park.

Aided by another successful set design by Tom John—a series of Plexiglas platforms on different levels—Streisand joked with the crowd and exhibited none of the nervousness she felt. Ultimately, the concert is memorable for two reasons. It was the first pop vocalist concert on this scale in Central Park, setting a precedent for other concerts that would follow over the next thirty-five years. Second, towards the end of the concert, there is one stunning artistic moment that serves to remind the viewer of Streisand's originality as an artist during this time. Speaking in a hushed voice that quieted the crowd, referring to the "lovely night . . . [which is] very sort of, in a strange way, peaceful," Streisand begins to sing "Silent Night." Unfurling her voice literally to the heavens above, it is a transcendent moment because Streisand has achieved a totally primal response in the crowd: It is as if, just for the three minutes of "Silent Night," all defenses and hostilities are suspended, a palpable yearning for peace—personal and international—is allowed to bloom. One almost feels the entire audience suspending its breath—or more precisely, one feels the entire audience breathing as one. The moment vanishes shortly thereafter—it is New York City after all. But for however short a time, a great artist has touched people's hearts in the most elemental way possible.

Her film career in full swing, it was to be five years before Streisand fulfilled her commitment to CBS for a final television special. Entitled *Barbra Streisand and Other Musical Instruments,* it was filmed in London and aired in November 1973. In a word: strange.

One of the interesting things about great popular artists is that when they go off the tracks they do so in spectacular fashion, and yet so strong is the pull of their personality that they continue to exert their fascination. This is precisely what happened with *Barbra Streisand and Other Musical Instruments,* for at the end of the show, one is again left wondering: "*What* was she thinking?"

After a nice beginning with "Sing/Make Your Own Kind of Music," and some genuinely funny comic musical byplay with eleven-year-old pianist Dominic Savage, the first act degenerates into a nearly fifteen-minute medley of standards sung in exotic musical settings: a kabuki "Glad to Be Unhappy," tom-toms for "Don't Rain on My Parade." Yes, there are some interesting visual images, but the entire exercise is mostly unlistenable. Rhythms and melody lines are distorted beyond recognition—no famous composer would have supplied liner notes for a CD of these versions.

Act II contains a genuinely fine duet with the legendary Ray Charles on "Cryin' Time," and is welcome proof positive of Streisand's genuine respect for great artists. Never pulling focus from Charles, indeed singing backup for him on "Look What They've Done to My Song"; the admiration she obviously feels for such a great artist shines through as clearly as it did when she worked with Garland and Louis Armstrong. Unfortunately, this second act also contains silly special effects, a gimmicky truncated version of "Don't Ever Leave Me" (part of a loneliness-themed musical sequence), an uninspired "comic" monologue, and a toned-down version of "Sweet Inspiration/Where You Lead," famous and Grammy-nominated from the *Live Concert at the Forum* album. Here the medley contains no horns, no fast hand-clapping, and no approximation of her rock-and-roll voice—just a bland, syrupy vocal lacking in any energy.

The weirdest part of all was yet to come. Echoing the format of the previous television specials, the final act was a concert. First up: a sing-along version of Schubert's "Auf dem Wasser zu singen." Hello?! Doubtless viewers all over America eagerly followed the bouncing ball on top of the lyrics . . . Unfortunately, the absolute low point of the entire multi-million-dollar affair followed shortly thereafter: the concept medley entitled "The World Is a Concert," which featured Barbra singing against the everyday sounds of a vacuum cleaner, juicer, steam kettle, and sewing machine. The mind boggles at the silliness of it all. At the early production meetings, did someone say "Hey—we've got the world's most popular female vocalist. Forget the time-tested standards and a full orchestra. Let's really give them what they want— Barbra accompanied by a vacuum cleaner. Blenders! That's the ticket. And let's have Barbra's manager Martin Erlichman playing the washing machine. That'll really make for a great show."

In the end, the special proved to be a gimmicky, artificial prime-time hour devoid of all the wit and originality displayed in her first two specials. With exactly one exception. In the middle of the concert segment, Barbra, in a long white gown, sang the Harold Arlen/Truman Capote ballad "I Never Has Seen Snow." No gimmicks, no flash. Just a singer (a singer? Hell—*the* female singer), her favorite composer, a full orchestra, and five minutes and four seconds of great popular singing. It was too little too late, but served as a potent reminder of just how good Streisand could be. The special ended with a gauzily filtered Barbra singing Richard Rodgers' "The Sweetest Sounds." Nice vocal, but the visual was just as out of focus as the preceding fifty-eight minutes. Not as bad as *The Belle of 14th Street,* but not that much better, *Barbra Streisand and Other Musical Instruments* stands as the first true waste of Streisand's talent—power and total artistic control were hers, and washing machines were the best she came up with.

Having fulfilled her contractual obligations to CBS, Streisand never again appeared in a themed television special. Audience tastes changed, primarily due to the growth of cable television and the loosening of the big three networks' hold on viewers. No longer did an artist have to try to appeal to the broadest possible audience because of the entire nation watching only three channels. Instead, with the public choosing among dozens of channels, performers were free to present themselves unfettered, as it were, and that is exactly what Streisand did over the next thirty years. Solo concerts proved the order of her day, and HBO, the premiere pay cable channel, was only too willing to film her 1986 *One Voice* concert for future telecast.

One Voice marked Streisand's first public concert in over a decade, and even more to the point, it marked a turning point in her career and the public's perception of her. The concert came about in reaction to the nuclear disaster at Chernobyl and had the avowed purpose of raising enough money to help the Democrats take back control of the U.S. Senate. With the *One Voice* concert, the blending of the artistic and the political moved front and center in Streisand's career. She would raise her "one voice" to help raise money and public consciousness, and show that "one voice" could make a difference. Streisand's concern over political issues, her anger with the Republican Reagan administration then in power, grew so intense that it actually overcame her by-now legendary stage fright. To people who wanted her to "just shut up and sing," as Laura Ingraham titled her 2003 book, well, Barbra's response was, in effect, "Tough shit."

The decision to overtly politicize her work made Barbra extremely controversial and developed into a motif that colored all subsequent press coverage and response to her. For the vast majority of Americans, Stresiand's liberal politics could no longer be separated from her singing—not since the days of "Hanoi Jane" Fonda opposing the Vietnam War had a movie star proven so controversial. In fact, the politicization of her work, from this 1986 concert onward, has remained a constant in her career and in the press coverage pertaining thereto. In reality, it now rivals talk of her obsessive perfectionism as the most commented-upon aspect of her extraordinary career. Lost in all of the political hubbub was the fact that the *One Voice* concert was a damn good evening of singing; after years of public silence, the Streisand magic remained undiminished.

In retrospect it is amusing to note that in the then newly inaugurated video age, Streisand found a way to update the concept of admiring album liner notes from legendary composers; instead of Richard Rodgers and Harold Arlen writing words of praise, the *One Voice* special opened with the HBO cameras capturing a virtual who's who of the biggest stars in Hollywood singing Barbra's praises. Henry Winkler: "I think that it is enormous that Barbra Streisand said she would sing in public for the first time in years." Bette Midler, who throughout the years has alternated between praising Streisand's talent and denigrating her obsessive traits and high-priced concert tickets (pricing at which Midler herself is no slouch) was, for the purposes of *One Voice,* in praise mode: "I've never seen her live and a lot of people here haven't seen her live . . . So it's a real—how do you say—a double treat."

The stage set: a special outdoor ampitheater constructed on the grounds of Barbra's Malibu estate for the concert. Three hundred powerful luminaries: A visibly nervous Robin Williams opened the concert, joking that his entire career could be made or destroyed by those in attendance at the concert: "This is scary . . . My entire career is floating before me. You see people here who can say, 'I don't like him. Get someone else.'"

At last, with a flourish of dry ice, that familiar voice began to sing, "There's a place for us, somewhere a place for us," and the backlit diva made her entrance to thunderous applause. It was a concert entrance delayed for over a decade, and yet seemingly as natural as when the fearless teenager first conquered New York City armed only with a superior voice and enough chutzpah to power the entire subway system.

The concert played like an evening of Streisand's greatest hits, with patter and songs specifically geared to the political and environmental causes of the evening. The beauty of nature—"Evergreen." The danger of nuclear disaster threatening life on earth—"People." The hopes of a better life and the most public take on a Judy Garland classic—a sweetly sung "Over the Rainbow" dedicated to Garland. Although joined by Barry Gibb for "Guilty" and "What Kind of Fool," the evening was really all Barbra's, most powerfully so in a candlelit version of "Papa, Can You Hear Me?," dedicated to political father figures: Gandhi, John Kennedy, Anwar Sadat.

There were special lyrics to "Send in the Clowns," poking fun at the Republicans: "Aren't they rich? Aren't they queer?" and a sense of hopefulness evident in both another Garland classic, "It's a New World," and an upbeat "Happy Days Are Here Again." Sounding in great voice, nary a stumble no matter how difficult the tune, the evening ended on a triumphant political note, with Streisand leading the audience in "America the Beautiful." Streisand deliberately wanted to make the point that liberals can be and are every bit as patriotic as conservatives—and by the way, casually demonstrate that it's not your everyday diva who can lead Bette Midler and Whitney Houston in a sing-along patriotic anthem. The show garnered terrific reviews and stellar ratings for HBO. The concert raised $1.5 million dollars and five of the six Democratic senatorial candidates were triumphant. The cross-pollination was now not just music and film—it was music, film, and politics. The gauntlet was laid down. What next?

Concerts

Nothing that Streisand has ever done—no recording, no movie, no previous concert or stage appearance—can touch what she accomplishes in her serene maturity. Standing on the Madison Square Garden stage, sleek and gleaming, she is the pure distillation of what it means to be a show business genius.

—Liz Smith, *The New York Post*, June 22, 1994

Working with much less frequency, Streisand devoted years to directing, producing, and starring in *The Prince of Tides*. Album releases tended to be compilations with one or two new songs thrown in to entice the public, and after the triumphant release of *The Prince of Tides,* all was quiet until the bombshell announcement: For the first time since the 1972 concert at the Forum, Barbra Streisand would perform live in an arena for the general paying public. The occasion? A 1993 New Year's Eve concert in Las Vegas. The Eagle had landed.

It's a measure of how pent-up the desire was to see Streisand live that phone circuits actually overloaded from desperate callers trying to obtain tickets, with over one million calls made on the first day of ticket sales. (According to the *New York Times,* five million calls were logged when tickets for the New York City concerts went on sale.) The record-high ticket prices ($50 to $1,000) did nothing to stop Barbra's older, moneyed crowd from obsessing over the need to see her. (Lost in all of the talk about Barbra's $14 million payday for the two concerts was the fact that $3 million dollars was donated to charities of her choice.) By shrewdly waiting until the demand was at its peak, and her voice still in extraordinary condition, Streisand had guaranteed a frenzied reaction before she ever sang a note. Her reasons for concertizing were both practical and personal: practical because although extremely wealthy, Streisand's assets were property and equity heavy but cash light, and she wanted a big payout. At the same time, there were personal reasons as well; in a lifetime spent overcoming obstacles, Barbra wanted to overcome her fear of live performing. After the first concert on New Year's Eve, true to form, she rehearsed for hours the next day to iron out the perceived flaws. When the second concert proved a triumph not only for the crowd (who would have cheered if she had coughed for two hours) but also for Streisand herself, even by her own notoriously tough perfectionist standards, the decision was made: A full-scale concert tour would ensue.

Of course, this meant full-scale by Barbra's standards, not by industry standards. Barbra would conceive, write, direct, and produce the show herself. No detail would escape her attention, right down to the 16,500 square feet of carpeting installed in each arena in order to ensure better sound. Interestingly, glossed over in the avalanche of news about the concert was the fact that this "full-scale" tour would consist of twenty-six concerts over a period of five months in six cities: London, Detroit, Washington D.C., San Jose, Anaheim, and New York. This, compared to Cher's three-year-long "farewell tour" of more than three hundred concerts. No matter. After a successful "tryout" (?!) in London before Prince Charles, Elton John, and the like, after a return to Detroit, the site of her first-ever out-of-town singing engagement, after a hit in Bill Clinton–era Washington, D.C., Barbra Streisand arrived back in her hometown of New York City, and proceeded to rack up the biggest single triumph of her entire storied career.

> *Barbra Streisand, complete with her orchestra, its deep*
> *arrangements, and her tall, layered voice, has been advancing*
> *on New York like the Roman legions on Gaul. . . .*
> —Whitney Balliett, *The New Yorker*, June 20, 1994

Both live and in the HBO televised version of the concert, Streisand was at her peak, so downright brilliant both in simple and complex terms that one was tempted to ask, "What the hell took you so long?" But then, everyone knew the answers—the stage fright, the perfectionism, the . . . it didn't matter. Barbra was home.

After a thunderous Broadway-style overture of her greatest hits played by a sixty-four-piece orchestra, Barbra appeared on the balcony level of the white Georgian-inspired set—a vision in white. After a tumultuous standing ovation, the first words she sang publicly in New York City after twenty-seven years told the story:

> *I don't know why I'm frightened*
> *I know my way around here.*

The special lyrics to Andrew Lloyd Webber and Don Black's "As If We Never Said Goodbye" from *Sunset Boulevard* continued to unfurl, gathering strength, until, in full voice, before fifteen thousand adoring fans, Barbra Streisand sang,

> *Now I'm standing center stage*
> *I've come home at last.*

It wasn't just the standing ovation at these words mid-song. It was the fact that Barbra, the Brooklyn girl made good, the Broadway baby, New-Yorker-to-the-bone-no-matter-how-long-she-lives-in-L.A., had come home to her people. These were New Yorkers who loved her not in spite of her blunt manner, in-your-face attitude, left-leaning political opinions, and I'm-great-and-we-all-know-it-so-step-aside style, but *because* of it. Barbra Streisand was triumphing, making it happen live for every person in the live audience (and in the subsequent television audience) who ever wanted to shout out, "You're gonna hear from me!" And she did it with unadulterated brilliance— the biggest artistic and personal success of her career.

The triumph proved so persuasive because it called on all of the

**THE TRIUMPHANT RETURN
TO THE CONCERT STAGE, 1994.** *CORBIS*

skills Streisand had developed as singer, actor, director, and producer. As Jon Pareles pointed out in his *New York Times* rave review of June 22, 1994, she seemed to reveal herself in the segments depicting sessions with her psychiatrist, yet actually revealed nothing at the rawest emotional level. She gave the crowd the illusion of intimacy with their idol, but in reality kept the twenty-seven-year air of mystery intact.

Constructed around themes that mattered to Streisand, the show connected her to the crowd in a way that a mere greatest hits run-through never could have. Touching on her Broadway roots ("Don't Rain on My Parade"), she sang of her career-defining themes: the longing for love, the need to belong, and lost love. The ultimate romantic singer constructed these themes as three-act plays—beginning, middle, end—singing "Will He Like Me"—"He Touched Me"—"Evergreen"—"The Man That Got Away"—again the connection to Judy Garland. "Ah," the audience seemed to say, "she hasn't forgotten. She's still one of us." Standing ovations ensued and then the directorial stroke: Dialogue about personal triumph, about growing as a person, and expanding vision led into "On a Clear Day," and as the song built, the jumbo screens flanking the stage flashed alive for the first time, the crowd screaming its approval. They may have been in the rafters of Madison Square Garden, but the screen close-up connected them intimately with Barbra, and as her voice soared to the final bell-like sounds of "You can see forever—Forever—For—e—ver—More," with the note held and held—the audience exploded. She was theirs. And more to the point, they were hers.

With the audience in the palm of her hand, and the video screen now working full-time, Director Streisand went to work. Act II began with screen footage from *Funny Girl* and *The Way We Were,* the ne plus ultra of her best screen acting *and* career-long pursuit of gorgeous Prince Charmings in the persons of Omar Sharif and Robert Redford. Signature song "The Way We Were" segued into Broadway songs "Lazy Afternoon" and Sondheim's "Not While I'm Around," complete with footage of son Jason Gould in *The Prince of Tides.* A personal connection with Barbra's family—and yet, cannily enough, nothing was truly revealed.

Reasserting the tone of hope with the new song "Ordinary Miracles," Streisand then launched into the peak of the concert, a medley of *Yentl* complete with film clips. Upon further examination, what becomes clear is that the four songs from *Yentl* constitute a nearly perfect summary of Streisand's life, career, and appeal to the masses. To wit: "Where Is It Written?"—the questions she has continually asked when breaking down barriers, barriers about "funny-looking" girls with show biz dreams, barriers about women taking control of their own careers. "Papa, Can You Hear Me?"—the neverending void without a father, the drive to make him proud and make her mother notice her, love her—childhood issues for the whole damn world. "Will Someone Ever Look at Me That Way?"—Barbra and every outsider yearning for Prince Charming, the Prince Charming who would be hers if only he

knew the *real* person. And finally, the thundering "A Piece of Sky"—
Barbra dueting with her screen image, the two Barbras harmonizing.
This is Yentl off to the new world of America as well as Brooklyn-born
Barbra off to conquer the new worlds of Manhattan and Hollywood—
make that off to conquer America. For every person in the audience
who ever wanted to soak up life and leave their mark:

> *What's wrong with wanting more?*
> *Why fly when you can soar?*
> *Why settle for just a piece of sky?*

Working on every conceivable level, the medley left even the older,
monied crowd—no rock concert this—on its feet literally screaming
its approval.

The finishing touches were put on the concert with a joyful, triumphant "Happy Days Are Here Again" sung to video footage of
Clinton-era politics: Nelson Mandela, the crumbling of the Berlin
Wall, a woman's right to choose—of course the political would be in-
corporated, and of course Bill Clinton would be praised. The encores
began with signature song "My Man," continued with the languid yet
pointed "For All We Know" ("For all we know we may never meet
again"—well, if it took twenty-seven years for this concert, she might
be right), and then the capper: the Sondheim/Bernstein "Somewhere"
from *West Side Story,* introduced with the words, "My idea of a perfect
world is one in which we really appreciate each other's differences—
short, tall, Democrat, Republican, black, white, gay, straight—a world
in which all of us are equal but definitely not the same, right?!" Propelled by Barbra's surging voice, the song has been rethought since
the electronic *Broadway Album* version and the *One Voice* concert
opener: this is the finale, and she is singing directly to every person
who ever felt they didn't belong, saying we're in it together; we can
all make it:

Hold my hand and we're halfway there
Hold my hand and I'll take you there
Somehow
Someday . . .

and then a slowed-down, belted, descending three-note

So-o-ome-where.

Triumphant.

The Concert represented a perfectionist vision presented live but preserved on film. Millions earned. Her best reviews in decades. Hundreds of thousands of happy fans who saw her live. A top-ten platinum certified CD recording. A top-rated HBO special. Millions of television viewers. Two Emmy Awards: Best Special, Best Individual Achievement in Performance. No way to top it. Seemingly she never will.

When New Year's Eve 1999 rolled around, Streisand broke her five-and-one-half-year concert silence to ring in the millennium with a *Timeless* concert at the MGM Grand Hotel in Vegas. The reasoning behind it, once again, was twofold: the opportunity to make millions of dollars for two concerts, and the chance to bid farewell to live performing with one last grandly conceived concert. These Vegas millennium concerts on New Year's Eve and New Year's Day quickly sold out at sky-high prices, and resulted in Streisand scheduling four final farewell concerts, two in Los Angeles, and finally, two in New York City. Sandwiched in between were concerts in Sydney, Australia, but New York City, where it all began, was where her live performing career would end. Forever.

BYE, BYE BARBRA! A CITY'S VERKLEMPT
—Headline in *The New York Observer* regarding the final concerts,
October 2, 2000

New York is my home, regardless of where my house is.
—Barbra Streisand, before the final concerts in 2000

Once again, the shows would be conceived, directed, produced by, and starring Streisand herself. The shows would also be filmed for future telecast on HBO. After the enormous success of the 1994 concerts, hopes were high that these would even top those career-defining evenings. Only Barbra could top "The Concert." Only Barbra could improve on those historic nights. Could she? Would she?

She didn't. And in many ways, it didn't really matter. Maybe it was Streisand's self-professed happiness from her marriage to James Brolin. Maybe the personal happiness blunted the edge of her perfectionist drive. She no longer *had* to show the world. Whatever the reason, a relaxed, confident Streisand put on concerts that seemed almost casual compared with the elegant lines, look, and sounds of the 1994 events. (There was, however, nothing casual about the $2,500 top ticket price, or the sixty-two-piece orchestra.) For anyone else these farewell evenings would have been unadulterated triumphs. For Streisand they simply suffered by comparison to her own 1994 achievements.

Because of the farewell nature of the concerts, these evenings were scripted along the chronological, autobiographical lines of "And then I sang/acted/wrote/directed/produced." The problem was that although the audience was happy to hear such a greatest hits recital, there was no sense of discovery, no shared journey or insights, which is the path great artists lead us along.

The evening opened with a rather unnecessary tap dance appearance by Savion Glover as Father Time, dancing the clock back to 1955 and the thirteen-year-old Barbra Joan cutting her first demo record with her mother. Dialogue between Diana Kind (Randee Heller) and young Barbra (lookalike Lauren Frost) established both the nagging mother motif and Barbra's refusal to listen, but this established vocabulary came at some cost. By the time Barbra herself appeared to the thundering percussive beat of "Something's Coming," the audience, although primed for the obligatory standing ovation, seemed almost puzzled. Who was that tap dancer in a cape? Barbra's mother—what she's doing here? Oddly enough, these very autobiographical touches felt much less personal and revealing than the 1994 concert opening lines of "I don't know why I'm frightened. I know my way around here."

This time around, Barbra herself appeared looser and more confident—a reaction she admitted was a combination of having a good time *and* knowing that she wouldn't have to sing in public any longer. But—the resulting lack of tension meant that the evening had lost its edge. The evening wasn't an event—just a very good concert.

What followed in Act I was a by-the-numbers chronological rendering of Streisand's career. The Bon Soir—"Cry Me a River"; Basin Street East—"A Sleepin' Bee"; Broadway—*Wholesale* and *Funny Girl;* The movies—"Evergreen." THAT VOICE was still present, and still present in capital letters, but none of it was new. Not until the Act I closer of the *Yentl* medley did Streisand surprise. Familiar with the medley from the 1994 concerts, the audience edged forward in its seats, the atmosphere transformed with electricity, and then Streisand pulled off a directorial coup and indeed topped herself; video screens running, the pounding Broadway-esque sounds of "A Piece of Sky" filling the air, Barbra not only sang with her *Yentl* screen self, but also with her young thirteen-year-old self, played by Lauren Frost. Turning in unison from left to right, young Barbra, onscreen Barbra, and present-day Barbra herself all belted out the final notes—with maybe the adult Barbra holding the note an extra bit longer, just to let everyone know—and the crowd was on its feet, screaming approval. For this one sequence, Barbra had managed to top herself, and hadn't that been a driving force behind the entire career?

Hers has been a career built on telling herself—telling everyone—that when what you're reaching for what is just over the horizon, the only way you'll get there is to try harder, to keep showing everyone, to keep topping yourself. Only now, Barbra really had made it to that fairytale ending, professionally and personally. And—no real surprise—the exciting tension, the heightened drama of it all, had been diminished.

Act II actually proved a sloppier act, redeemed by a slam-bang ending. Her sure-shot directorial touch was missing this time around. A terrific video career compilation, edited to within a milisecond of its life, first used when accepting her Grammy Legend award, was a guaranteed crowd pleaser, and a great start to Act II, but Streisand's entrance was off by a beat or two, negating the impact. Similarly, a sequence of duets proved nothing more than pleasant filler, and a rare Barbra concert was not supposed to be about pleasant filler. Celine Dion, Neil Diamond, and Barry Gibb were present only on video, Judy Garland and Frank Sinatra were no longer alive—what was the point? The forgettable disco song "The Main Event" was trotted out, complete with awkward choreography and three backup singers who never appeared again. It was almost as if Barbra the notorious perfectionist had improvised the rather haphazard sequencing of the songs.

Streisand's real-life fairytale happy ending was represented by video footage of husband James Brolin and two somewhat forgettable songs from the *A Love Like Ours* CD: "I've Dreamed of You" and "At the Same Time." The physical set was stunning (a vaguely Egyptian-meets-space-age motif), the orchestra lush and three-score strong, the voice superb, but the Act II material—*eh*.

But the finale—well, two finales really—these finales to her live performances redeemed all. The first included a melting "Don't Like Goodbyes"—superior even to the 1960s version on the *People* album—followed by a combination of "I Believe" and "Somewhere." These were songs that resonated musically, showed off her voice, and connected the star with her devoted audience on a personal level. Streisand believes in the old romantic myths—after all, she made them come true in her own life, didn't she? She believes that somewhere there's a better world, and at her most personally involved best, she takes the audience, here fifteen-thousand strong, along for the ride towards that happy ending.

The second finale involved signature song "My Man," and the surprising and inspired choice of "Before the Parade Passes By." Usually belted as the "Look at Me" Act I closer from *Hello, Dolly!,* it was here sung pensively as a meditation on wanting a personal life more than a performing life. And last, fittingly, a heartfelt "People." Her song for her fellow New Yorkers—and really for all those yearning for love and a sense of acceptance. As with all great artists, it was that simple and yet also that complex. As E. M. Forster wrote: "Only connect."

Theater

I'd give anything to be able to sing like you.

> —Sophia Loren, reportedly, to Barbra Streisand, backstage during the run of *Funny Girl*

If I looked like you, I wouldn't open my mouth.

> —Barbra Streisand's reported response to Sophia Loren

There is only one way to deal with Barbra Streisand: Tell her the truth. If you don't tell the truth then you're going to have problems.

> —Jule Styne, Composer, *Funny Girl*

From the start, Barbra Streisand had her eye set on stardom, and that meant movie stardom. Like a general planning an invasion—in this case the invasion of Hollywood by a very different-looking, very ethnic girl—Streisand launched an all-stops-out assault on live appearances, records, and theater as a means to that end. Upon obtaining the goal of movie stardom, theater could be jettisoned, but in the beginning, Streisand viewed theater as the way to prove she could act; even then she saw herself not as a singer, but as an actress who sings. In her eyes it was simple. Singing was a gift she possessed, a gift for which she was fairly grateful, but one whose value lay in the fact that it could get her roles in theater, which would lead to starring roles, which would lead to Oz, a.k.a. Hollywood.

It therefore makes a curious kind of sense when one realizes that this icon, forever identified with New York City and Broadway musicals, had an extraordinarily brief theatrical career as a professional actress: three shows in four and one half years. 1961–1966. End of story. Over and out. And no more theater work for forty years and counting.

First up were two very quick flops: *The Insect Comedy,* a satire written in 1921 that lasted three performances in May 1960. Barbra as, among other roles, a moth and a butterfly. Next up was *Another Evening with Harry Stoones,* a one-night run, October 21, 1961. In a cast that included Dom DeLuise and Diana Sands, Streisand sang

MISS YETTA TESSYE MARMELSTEIN, WALLFLOWER ON WHEELS.
I CAN GET IT FOR YOU WHOLESALE, 1963. *SPRINGER/PHOTOFEST*

"Value"—later resurrected for the 1967 concert in Central Park. Did she like theater work? Yes—but. Next time it had to be uptown. Broadway. It was.

I Can Get It For You Wholesale: Barbra as frumpy, unattractive secretary Yetta Tessye Marmelstein. Stopping the show nightly. And for the general public, the Broadway legend began. But amongst theater professionals, the legend began at the audition for *Wholesale.* Present at the audition were powerful theater professionals David Merrick, Herb Ross, Harold Rome, and Arthur Laurents. And what did this untested neophyte do? Was she scared witless? Not a chance. First she unfurled her music like an accordion, three songs taped together, music hurtling across the floor. The strange-looking creature definitely had their attention now. Singing three songs, including "Value," she impressed them enough to be given the music to "Miss Marmelstein" and was told to learn it for an audition a few hours later. And like all legends, here is where the different versions of the story begin.

Was there a mobile secretary's chair onstage? Did Barbra take out chewing gum and stick it underneath the chair before launching into song? Streisand says yes. Director/librettist Laurents says no. Audacious. No matter. This strange-looking, skinny young girl with inches-long fingernails and purple lipstick sang in a voice so true that a part written for a fifty-year-old woman became the property of a nineteen-year-old tyro.

Rehearsals. Arguments with the veteran, well-respected Laurents (author of *West Side Story* and *Gypsy*—only two of the all-time great Broadway musicals). He—determined to tone her down. She was great—he knew it—but also all over the place. Too much of everything—too many "take-ums" in the words of Laurents himself. She—determined to stand out from the ensemble. As if the ensemble had a chance. A four-minute solo on the mobile secretary's chair. Never stopping the movement or the hilarious Brooklyn-flavored patter and song. Arguments abounded with the musical director, the veteran Lehman Engel. Compromise. Result: stopping the show on a nightly basis. The show may have had mediocre reviews but there were raves for Barbra. Photo articles in *LIFE, Look, Time.* Great. Now, about that starring role . . .

And that starring role came down the pike in the form of *Funny Girl*—the story of Jewish comedienne/singer Fanny Brice, a native New Yorker who overcame her oddball looks to triumph in show business. Sound like anyone else you've heard of? And, contrary to myth, the role didn't just present itself—Streisand and her ever-valuable manager Martin Erlichman heard about the proposed musical biography and pursued it relentlessly. Barbra knew this was the role of a lifetime, and like a runaway locomotive, fixed her eye on the horizon, full steam ahead.

In retrospect the choice of Streisand as Fanny Brice appears inevitable, but at the time, it seemed anything but. Mary Martin? Carol Burnett? Eydie Gormé? Most seriously, Anne Bancroft. Streisand's inner pilot told her that only she could play the part properly, and the systematic wooing of the power players involved revealed the full extent of just what could be accomplished by her extraordinary combination of huge talent and overwhelming ambition. Talent and chutzpah: the two constants in her career throughout the decades. Everybody said no, we don't want her as Fanny Brice. Well then, one by one Streisand would show them; when her star had been firmly established by her overwhelming triumph on Broadway, Barbra herself was not above embellishing these struggles, thereby burnishing the legend and endearing herself to her fans all the more.

First on board—composer Jule Styne. He saw her twenty-seven out of twenty-eight nights at the Bon Soir, becoming totally convinced that only Streisand could play the role. Even more to the point, he convinced himself that with THAT VOICE on board, he could score with some big fat hit songs. Sold. Next on board—erstwhile nemesis David Merrick (*Wholesale* producer), then attached as co-producer with Brice's son-in-law Ray Stark. Next up—director Garson Kanin and wife, Ruth Gordon, with Gordon purportedly won over by the sheer force of Streisand's voluble Brooklyn personality. Hardest of all to convince—Ray Stark and especially his wife, Fran, Brice's daughter. Fran Stark, convinced that Streisand utterly lacked her mother's inherent elegance, remained violently opposed to casting Barbra. But, with the others now in the Streisand camp, Fran Stark's unwillingness to acquiesce became harder to justify, and in the end, the part was Barbra's. First by singing, then by force of personality, she had bulldozed all obstacles in front of her. Not a bad metaphor for her career.

Legend has it that once the part was hers, Streisand sailed through effortlessly by sheer dint of her talent. But, like so many legends, it is not true. From the start of the contentious rehearsal period, Streisand's singing soared. Jule Styne, galvanized by the opportunities she presented, began to write more and more music (he claimed to have written fifty-five pieces of music for the show by the time it opened). But—but—as the show tried out in Philadelphia and Boston, Streisand the inexperienced actress floundered in the book scenes. The problem was solved in classic Streisand fashion: learn and take what she could from everyone possible. If feelings were hurt along the way, too bad. It wasn't done with malice, but this was business. Nothing would interfere. And it didn't.

Director Garson Kanin (soon to be fired), Ruth Gordon, bookwriter Isobel Lennart (who termed working on the project an "ego-crushing experience"), Peter Daniels, Jule Styne, arranger Luther Henderson, personal acting coach Alan Miller—she took from all of them. Newly hired production supervisor and theater legend Jerome Robbins? She'd go toe to toe with him, but respecting the breadth and depth of his knowledge, soaked up everything she could (thirty years later, introducing him at her 1994 concerts, she simply referred to him as "a genius"). She'd show them all, damn it. Knowing that the role of Fanny Brice presented a once-in-a-lifetime opportunity which would give her the chance to sing, clown, and wring pathos—the triple crown on Broadway—she'd make it work.

And she did. They all did, because bit by bit, beat by beat, a character emerged. Fanny Brice onstage, a recognizable figure, complex, alive, and, well, fascinating. Taking from them all, learning from them all, she *could* do it all.

Which is when and how the most consistent and powerful strain of career criticism—of gossip even—began to emerge around the twenty-two-year-old, a criticism that has continued unabated for four decades. Namely, she was power hungry. She wouldn't listen. How dare this woman—this *girl*—act like that? Wasn't she grateful for the chance? She should listen to older, more experienced hands who knew better. Except she didn't think they knew better. Yes, they had more experience, but *she* was the one onstage nonstop for two and one half hours. She had her butt on the line, and they also better listen to her.

> *She carries her own spotlight.*
>
> —Jule Styne, Composer, *Funny Girl*

Rumors circulated that Streisand saw to it that other roles were cut back, making sure the focus was on Barbra, Barbra, Barbra. It may have been true—but the creators' decision to do so also came out of the knowledge that the show seemed to die whenever she wasn't the focus, spurting blazingly back to life when she launched into song or comedy. Without Barbra front and center, *Funny Girl* plotzed onstage like the stereotypical, sanitized (remember Fran Stark) show business bio it was. With Barbra front, center, and alone in the followspot, that unique Broadway musical-theater magic ignited. After all the tumult in Philadelphia and Boston, the hirings, the firings, the drama of it all, when Barbra's final notes soared into the rear of the Winter Garden Theater on the opening night of March 26, 1964, when those jaded New Yorkers heard the words

> *Nobody—no nobody is gonna*
> *Rain on my parade . . .*

the place exploded. The world of show business was hers. New York was hers.

Good. Fine. But what was next? Because Barbra Streisand very quickly became restless. She'd stay in the show for eighteen months if it would guarantee her the movie. She'd play the show in London if it guaranteed her the movie. But after the excitement of creating the show—forty-two versions of the final scene alone, the scene frozen only hours before the opening night curtain—after being so stimulated by the

REHEARSING *FUNNY GIRL,* THRIFT SHOP CLOTHES AND ALL, 1963.
SPRINGER/PHOTOFEST

constant changes and experimentation inherent in creating a show, Barbra began to feel trapped. Crossing off the days on a calendar, counting down the time remaining on her contract, because she wanted out. This Broadway stuff was nice, but real stardom meant movie stardom and after her final Broadway performance on December 26, 1965, she returned to the stage only for a three-month 1966 stint in the London production of *Funny Girl*. Raves followed in London, where an eerily prescient review by Herbert Kretzmer in the *London Express* synthesized the simultaneous blessing and curse that was already Barbra's at age twenty-two: "She performs the daunting feat of living up to the legend . . . The girl and the myth are indivisible."

Like every starstruck girl in America, Barbra wanted movie stardom. Unlike every starstruck girl in America, she'd make it happen. Forty years after her final performance in *Funny Girl* she has yet to give even one additional performance on a Broadway stage. With her eye on the target of Hollywood stardom, it was as if Sondheim had written the "Rose's Turn" lyric in *Gypsy* with Barbra Streisand in mind:

> *Startin' now it's gonna be my turn!*
> *Gangway, world,*
> *Get offa my runway!*

And most of the world did.

Politics

I'm a feminist, Jewish, opinionated, liberal woman. I push a lot of buttons.

—Barbra Streisand, 1996

With any superstar, after the burst of initial press coverage and the thrill of discovery (and it is a thrill for press and public alike, be it Sinatra, the Beatles, Elvis, or Streisand), the media coverage settles into definite patterns. Personal life details are endlessly trotted out, and the public's initial discovery of the icon settles into grooves that reinforce that early press. With Sinatra, the stories of tempestuous love affairs (Ava Gardner), the boozing, brawling, and rumored Mafia connections are all juxtaposed with the male vulnerability that came through so strongly in his "Only the Lonely" ballad singing. With Elvis, it was the young, sexy rock and roller, the white boy connected to black music, contrasted with the bloated, drugged-out Vegas superstar, constantly surrounded by an entourage. It was the Memphis Mafia for Elvis, and supposedly the Italian Mafia for Sinatra.

For Streisand, after the initial image of the Brooklyn kook, the coverage evolved in a slightly different manner that didn't focus solely on her personal life. Indeed, for all of the coverage of her love life (Canadian Prime Minister Pierre Trudeau to Jon Peters to Don Johnson to the much younger Andre Agassi), the press really focused on two disparate strands in her life. First, her obsession with perfectionism and absolute control of the creative process, and second, her political views. In fact, after her marriage to James Brolin, when Streisand's work activities seemed limited to one CD release per year, her name was still in the headlines only because of her political views.

Although an enormous amount of press has been generated by Barbra's political activities, what has been less frequently examined are the underlying reasons for her beliefs and increasingly outspoken positions on controversial issues. And, on a deeper level, how are these beliefs reflected in her professional projects, if they are at all?

First, and most strikingly, it would seem that her lifelong feeling of being an outsider has ensured her identification with fellow outsiders of all stripes. Mocked as strange-looking "crazy Barbra" when a little girl, Streisand, now the ultimate Hollywood power player, clearly has never regarded herself as an insider. At her 1995 Harvard University speech on politics, she referred to her disappointment and surprise at being embraced by the mainstream after her initial embrace by the more liberal, nontraditional urban denizens. This long-lasting self-perception of being an outsider fueled not only her strong connection with the gay community, but ensured her empathy with outcasts from mainstream society. In the most basic terms, this empathy translated into support for more liberal—i.e., Democratic—politicians.

In addition, just as Jacqueline Kennedy Onassis, the ultimate society insider, spoke of still always feeling like an outsider because of her Catholicism, Streisand's Jewishness has informed her sense of being marginalized, thereby affecting her political beliefs. Deemed outsiders by the same Protestant high society to which Mrs. Onassis referred, the majority of Jewish men and women in the United States have traditionally supported liberal policies and political parties. Streisand herself has spoken of her adherence to the Judaic concept of *tikkun olam*—the responsibility for repairing the world. In Barbra's case, these feelings may very well have been heightened by her difficult family life as a child: With no father, a distant, distracted mother, and an antagonistic stepfather, any child would of necessity ask herself, "Why don't I fit in? Are there others like me?" Such questions could be answered in one of two ways: by either desperately trying to join the establishment through embracing its mores and belief systems, or by going it alone, relying on an inner moral compass to chart one's path. Given the willfulness Barbra displayed even as a little girl—a little girl her own grandmother characterized as *farbrent* (Yiddish for "on fire")—there was no question which path Streisand would choose. To her credit, it is not a path she abandoned upon achieving success. If anything, it was at that point that her willingness to blaze her own trail became even more pronounced.

In discussing the influences upon her political thinking in a 1996 cover story in the political magazine *George,* Barbra herself stressed the lasting influence of her father. Having lost her father at age fifteen months, she did not know him, yet stressed the great influence he has continued to exert upon her thinking: "I feel like I am my father's daughter today. I am an extension of him."

Cast in the role of Hollywood's über-Democrat thanks to her fundraising concerts and strong connection to President Bill Clinton, Streisand's political evolution is usually ignored. In reality, the first political candidate she ever campaigned for was Republican New York City mayor John Lindsay. She supported Martin Luther King, Jr.'s Southern Christian Leadership Conference, and her relatively low-key involvement in Lindsay's mayoral campaign was followed by support for Bella Abzug—definitely not a low-profile candidate. Barbra, microphone in hand, campaigned next to Bella from a flatbed truck in the summer of 1970; the publicity the appearance generated helped Abzug triumph in a tightly contested Democratic primary and subsequently win election to the House of Representatives. The press noticed this support, and the subtext of the coverage, especially in middle America, said, in effect, "one loudmouthed Jewish broad supporting another." The first seeds of resentment amongst the more conservative elements in America were sown. This resentment became more widespread with Streisand's active participation in the 1972 presidential campaign of liberal Democrat George McGovern. The live recording of the concert fundraiser at the Forum on behalf of McGovern ensured that this political connection would live on in the public's mind long after the campaign was over, and Streisand found herself a self-proclaimed "proud" member of the infamous Nixon enemies list, as a result of her participation.

Although Streisand's liberal bona fides were well established by this time, she was relatively quiet on the political front during the late 1970s and early 1980s. This all changed with the 1986 accident at the Chernobyl nuclear power plant. Speaking with close friend Marilyn Bergman about the accident and related issues of nuclear disarmament led Barbra to join the Hollywood Women's Political Committee, and subsequently to the idea of a concert to raise money for the HWPC in support of Democratic senatorial candidates. Outspoken in her criticism of the Reagan White House, Streisand's 1986 *One Voice* concert (complete with an anti-Republican revised version of "Send in the Clowns" entitled "Send Home the Clowns") marked the turning point in coverage of Streisand. After the concert, the press and public perception of Streisand was almost always filtered through the lens of "diva as the ultimate Hollywood liberal." Those who derided her as a silly celebrity missed the very real point that a concert such as *One Voice* raised millions of dollars (seven million and counting as of March 2005), enough money to ensure that five of the six senators the HWPC supported were elected; at that point in the 1980s, those senators helped block the appointment of Robert Bork to the Supreme Court. Whether one agrees with her beliefs or not, taken to its logical conclusion, this action, as pointed out in the *George* cover story, helped ensure that Roe v. Wade would not be overturned—a very real demonstration of how Streisand's singing indirectly enabled her to exercise political influence.

The chronological listing of her fundraising concerts throughout the years reads like an honor roll of liberal Democratic candidates and causes: George McGovern—"Live Concert at the Forum," 1972; ACLU benefit—1980; HWPC—"One Voice" concert, 1986; Bill Clinton—1992 and 1996; Al Gore—2000; Democratic Congressional Campaign Committee—2002; John Kerry—2004. In other words, for the past three decades, only Barbra's political passion has proven stronger than her fear of performing live. It is no accident that the overwhelming majority of her website is devoted to political statements, writings, and essays, oftentimes couched in the strongest possible terms; with seemingly scant attention paid to news of her career, this represents a shift of priorities at first startling, and then remarkably consistent in tone and execution.

Streisand defied the "normal" human pattern of leading a more settled and conservative life as one grows older. In point of fact, as she aged and grew more comfortable in her own skin, she spoke out more frequently and with greater passion. And it wasn't just the speeches; unlike many celebrities, Barbra, in crude parlance, put her money where her mouth was. In 1990, after hearing about the imminent closing of a local Alaskan Public Radio station due to the economic downturn resulting from the Exxon Valdez oil spill, she sent enough money to keep the station on the air. In 1992, after the Los Angeles riots, she sent one hundred thousand dollars to area charities. At the time of the 1996 *George* magazine cover story on Streisand's political activism, she was publicly acknowleged as Hollywood's largest single celebrity donor to political campaigns. Contrary to the statements of her detractors, such generosity was not the result of a knee-jerk liberalism; clearly doing her homework and reading up on the issues, she even refused to give any money to the Democratic Senatorial Campaign Committee because they "distributed money to anti-choice Democrats in the South."

Still concerned with feminist issues, especially the place of women in Hollywood, at the 1992 Women in Film's Crystal Awards lunch, she gave a speech that not only addresssed problems faced by all women in the film industry, but which was phrased in language that clearly spoke to the very real problems she still faced, even in her position of enormous power and wealth: "A man is a perfectionist—a woman's a pain in the ass. He's committed—she's obsessed. If he acts, produces, and directs, he's called multi-talented. If she does the same thing, she's called vain and egotistical." It wasn't enough to sing special lyrics to "Putting It Together"—which addressed her own artistic struggles—she wanted to address the double standard in Hollywood in the strongest possible language, before an audience of her peers. Yes, this was a speech before a sympathetic audience, but it was still the sort of speech that could rankle powerful male executives in Hollywood, men who would look for an excuse to dismiss a project with a muttered, "What a pain in the ass. I don't want to greenlight her film." Still smarting from the criticism of her appearance and demeanor in *The Prince of Tides,* and in a neat foreshadowing of the criticism she'd receive for her dress at the Clinton pre-inaugural concert, she went on to state: "And I look forward to a society that . . . accepts the fact that a woman can be many, many things: strong *and* vulnerable, intelligent *and* sexy, opinionated *and* forgiving . . . They can get Ph.D.s *and* manicures." So there.

Words were not minced, and coupled with the fact that rather than limit herself to "safe" issues such as saving the rain forest, she spoke out repeatedly on the hot-button topic of gay rights and the battle against AIDS, Barbra became the chief celebrity bête noire of the far right. It wasn't just that she spoke out against Colorado's anti-gay Amendment 2 in 1992, urging other entertainers to consider boycotting Colorado. It was the fact that she spoke in blistering terms of former President Reagan's lack of response to the AIDS crisis. In 1992, at the gala "Commitment to Life VI" for AIDS Project LA, she termed his reaction a "genocidal denial" of the AIDS epidemic. Strong words, and ones from which she would not back down. Such passion infuriated her enemies even more, and at the same time, bolstered her core connection with her most ardent supporters.

This enmity reached new heights with the ascension of Bill Clinton to the White House in 1992. The bear-hug embrace with Clinton after singing at his inaugural gala further cemented this overtly political image. Streisand developed a very close, seemingly maternal friendship with Virginia Clinton Kelley, the President's mother, and in a very interesting and emotionally revealing photograph published in the souvenir program for her 1994 concerts, Barbra posed between her own mother, Diana Kind, and Virginia Kelley, holding hands with both women at the same time. Upon Mrs. Kelley's death, Streisand endowed a breast cancer research program in Kelley's name at the University of Arkansas Medical School, an action that could only have strengthened her connection with President Clinton.

Editorials were written about Streisand's closeness to the president, deriding both Streisand as an empty-headed Hollywood political wannabe and President Clinton for his too-enthusiastic embrace of Hollywood. The attacks on Barbra continued, even in a liberal publication such as the *New York Times* (in a bizarre op-ed piece by Anne Taylor Fleming on January 23, 1993, which criticized [the slit in] Streisand's skirt at the pre-inaugural concert as a "peekaboo power suit"). Conversely, and shortly thereafter, a letter to the editor of the *Times* praised Streisand for using her influence to help secure a million-dollar grant for Gay Men's Health Crisis. She remained a polarizing figure, no matter what the circumstances.

> *What the hell is Alan Greenspan doing raising the interest rates?*
> —Barbra Streisand's first words to CNN political analyst Bill
> Schneider, backstage immediately after her two-and-a-half
> hour solo concert in 1994

So strong was the press coverage of Streisand's political activity that rumors abounded that she would pursue a political office of her own; the *New York Post* of January 26, 1993 ran a front-page story—in very large type—bruiting about the possibility of "Senator Yentl." Streisand herself dismissed such speculation and, true to form, at one point spoke her mind in terms that would not endear any aspiring politician to the masses: "I don't want to go around shaking hands and having babies pee on me." Once a diva . . .

What was lost in the shuffle of loud press attention was one key element: For a nonelected entertainment-world figure, Streisand had obtained a position of artistic power and of access to political power rivaled in the history of Hollywood only by Frank Sinatra in the early days of the Kennedy administration. This was not just the power to bring a CD or movie to fruition—this was receiving-briefing-and-position-papers-from-the-White-House kind of power. Never mind the fact that President Clinton awarded Barbra the National Medal of the Arts; more noteworthy from the standpoint of influence was the fact that she was asked to join the governmental Health Care Task Force by powerful administration official Ira Magaziner. Criticized for not knowing enough about health-care issues, Barbra shot back that she had been asked to speak about communications and marketing, and that was something she did indeed know about. Any doubts about Streisand's access to the president were dispelled by Clinton administration insider George Stephanopoulos, who verified that Streisand occasionally spoke to the president about policy legislation, adding: "I don't want to give the impression that she's on the White House staff . . . But when the president speaks to her he values what she has to say."

Awareness of Streisand's liberal-icon status was ratcheted up several degrees by her February 3, 1995 speech on "The Artist as Citizen" at the John F. Kennedy School of Government at Harvard University. Television crews filmed the speech for cable broadcast, and the twin themes of her pride in being a liberal and the right of celebrities to be involved in politics served to infuriate the far right even more.

RECEIVING THE NATIONAL MEDAL OF THE ARTS FROM PRESIDENT CLINTON AT CONSTITUTION HALL AS BENNY CARTER, MIKHAIL BARYSHNIKOV, AND EDDIE ARNOLD LOOK ON. DECEMBER 20, 2000. *CORBIS*

> *I must admit that I'm confused by [House Speaker Gingrich's]*
> *thinking . . . He proposes taking children away from poor mothers and*
> *placing them in orphanages. If that's an example of mainstream culture, let*
> *me say I'm happy to be a member of the counterculture.*
> —Barbra Streisand, "The Artist as Citizen," speech
> at Harvard University, February 3, 1995

In front of an audience of students, professors, and the august likes of John Kenneth Galbraith, a visibly nervous Barbra Streisand delivered an effective speech, faltering only in the question-and-answer session, where she relied too often on a general answer: urging students to organize. Cogently arguing that an actor should not have to give up his or her role as citizen just because (s)he's in show business, she defended environmental protection and endowment of the arts and attacked the far right for "waging a war for the soul of America by making art a partisan issue." Most strongly of all, she ripped into the then all-powerful Speaker of the House, Newt Gingrich: "Is this a new Mc-Carthyism where Mr. Gingrich is suggesting that anyone who doesn't agree with him is abnormal?" She may have been nervous delivering the speech, but there was nothing tentative about her language. Whatever fright she felt when performing live, that fright never carried over into expressing her political opinions; by the time of the Clinton administration, she felt no compunction about tangling with either the media or the far right.

The very personal connection Streisand felt to then president Clinton during the 1990s could not be duplicated when Al Gore ran for president in 2000 or when John Kerry campaigned in 2004. Streisand dutifully sang at benefit concerts for both candidates, but at the Gore concert in 2000, the special lyrics to "Alfie" ("What's it all about, Albert?") rang hollow. It was similar to the difference she seemed to feel between singing for President Kennedy, whom she greatly admired ("He just glowed") and singing for President Lyndon Johnson at his 1965 inaugural ("a depressing evening"). With Presidents Kennedy and Clinton, both of whom were well read, smart, and charismatic, not to mention verbally adept, an instant personal connection was forged. To wit, Barbra's banter with President Kennedy after singing for him at the May 1963 Washington Press Correspondents Annual Dinner:

Barbra: "You're a doll."
President Kennedy: "How long have you been singing?"
Barbra: "As long as you've been president."

The successors to Kennedy and Clinton, i.e., Lyndon Johnson and Albert Gore, were strongly supported by Barbra over their Republican opponents, but the personal connection had vanished. It was never a question of which candidate Barbra would support in either the 2000 or 2004 presidential election. It was clear that she regarded George W. Bush as completely unfit for the office of president, and in a very controversial move, she sent a letter to Congressional Democrats in 2001 chastising them for being "paralyzed, demoralized, and depressed" since George W. Bush's inauguration. While she toned down the political criticism of Bush on her website in the aftermath of 9/11, with the passage of time, the anti-Bush comments returned in full force. In addition, a second controversial Streisand-penned statement reprimanding Democrats was sent to Senate Minority Leader Tom Daschle and House Minority Leader Richard Gephardt, one week before her appearance at the September 29, 2002, concert fundraiser for the Democratic Congressional Campaign Committee: "It is time for the Democrats to get off the defensive." Such statements were attacked by right and left alike, but not by the likes of Gephardt. He thanked her for the memo and stated that he and Barbra spoke regularly about politics. This was access to power, pure and simple.

> *I think we should send Barbra to Washington.*
> *At least she would properly pronounce* nuclear.
> —Barry Manilow, singer, at the September 29, 2002, fundraiser for
> the Democratic Congressional Campaign Committee

In the attacks on Streisand for daring to issue political missives complete with strategic advice, it was who-does-she-think-she-is time all over again. But a very interesting phenomenon emerged at the time of the 2004 presidential election. In the run-up to the election, Streisand's 2002 statements were exactly the sentiments increasingly worried Democratic politicians and supporters uttered, and in the hand-wringing and armchair analysis that dominated post-election discussions, right and left alike agreed that the defensive Democratic party had allowed the Republicans to set the tone and issues that framed

POLITICAL ACTIVIST: "THE ARTIST AS CITIZEN" SPEECH. CONSERVATIVES GROANED, LIBERALS CHEERED. HARVARD UNIVERSITY, FEBRUARY 3, 1995. *CORBIS*

the election. Ironically, the issues that seemed to dominate discussion at the time of the election were those about which Streisand felt most strongly: gay rights and a woman's right to choose.

The chorus of criticism from the right made Streisand the leading figure of celebrity derision in conservative circles—surpassing Tim Robbins and Susan Sarandon, Alec Baldwin, and even the Dixie Chicks, who had dared to criticize U.S. involvement in Iraq at the height of support for that war. Erstwhile liberals like Warren Beatty were noticeably circumspect—indeed silent—in their statements. In general terms, Beatty, at one time rumored to be interested in office himself, seemed to fall off the radar screen entirely, and chatted amiably with President Bush when honored at the Kennedy Center Honors in 2003. Conversely, it requires a real stretch of the imagination to picture Streisand chatting amiably with President Bush under any circumstances. Similarly, the formerly outspoken and cutting-edge Bette

Midler had long since settled into a safe, Disneyfied image, daring only by the standards of very conservative suburbia. Not so Streisand. The more she was criticized, the more she spoke out. The conservative press decided that the battle lines had been drawn. Laura Ingraham's conservative polemic *Shut Up and Sing* certainly seemed to have Streisand in mind with the book's title, and went on to excoriate Hollywood-style celebrity naiveté throughout the two-hundred-page broadside. For conservatives, Streisand, more than any other actor, became the symbol of every limousine liberal who was totally out of touch with the day to day problems faced by "real folk." Although the Republican candidates touted as being in touch with blue-collar concerns tended to be blue-blood WASPs to the manor born (e.g., George W. Bush), it was the born into straightened circumstances Streisand who was portrayed by conservatives as a rich actress/singer who didn't know what she was (loudly) talking about.

Aside from campaigning for candidates she supported, how then did Barbra's political passion actually manifest itself? The answer generally came in three forms: through television films she produced, through fundraising concerts, and by means of the Streisand Foundation. Applying her Hollywood clout to issue-oriented films she cared about, her production company, Barwood Films, produced the Emmy Award–winning *Serving in Silence: The Margarethe Cammermeyer Story* (NBC, 1995), the true-life story of a lesbian serving in the United States military. Barbra also executive produced a series of PBS specials about centenarians entitled *The Living Century* (2000), as well as the Lifetime lesbian-themed movie *What Makes a Family* in 2001.

If there was any other issue guaranteed to inflame the right as much as gay rights, it was gun control, a topic Barwood Films tackled in the 1998 NBC movie *The Long Island Incident*. The story of Carolyn McCarthy, a housewife on Long Island whose husband was killed (and son seriously injured) by a gunman on a suburban train at New York's Penn Station, the film detailed how McCarthy, outraged by what she deemed overly easy access to guns, ran for and was elected to Congress, fighting for new, tougher gun-control laws. True to form, these television films inspired both controversy and acclaim for Barbra, yet still served as rather strong retorts to those who had sneered, "Put your money where your mouth is." Agree or disagree with her, no one could say that she had not done exactly that.

On the non-work front, Streisand has endowed chairs in both women's studies and cardiovascular research, but her main vehicle for advancing social issues has been the Streisand Foundation, which funds work—ten million dollars worth as of March 2005—dedicated to those causes near to Streisand's heart: women's rights, AIDS research, civil liberties, and environmental protection. Board members have included son Jason Gould, ex-boyfriend Richard Baskin, and good friends Marilyn and Alan Bergman. Millions have been distributed and land has even been donated; the Santa Monica Mountain Conservancy received Barbra's twenty-four-acre Malibu estate, complete with five houses, a generous move that also provided Barbra with a multi-million dollar tax deduction.

She wouldn't play by the established entertainment-world rules in terms of looks, repertoire, or dress back in the 1960s, and she wouldn't "shut up and sing" in the first decade of the new millennium. What is less overt, but running beneath the surface nonetheless, is the belief that this loudmouthed Jewish broad just doesn't know her place.

Is this criticism of Streisand anti-Semitic? Possibly.

Is it sexist? Probably.

Is it anti–blue state/big city, i.e., anti–New York and Los Angeles? Definitely.

Is it anti all of the liberal political views she unabashedly espouses, among them a woman's right to choose and gay rights? Unquestionably.

Yet will the criticism stop her from speaking out? It never has and seemingly never will, because as she has stated on more than one occasion, she is simply not afraid of the criticism. The criticism may sting, but it provokes in her anything but fear. Ironically, it is this lack of fear in her political beliefs and statements that makes her feature film work (not the television movies she produces) from the past fourteen years frustrating to watch and nothing less than a disservice to her artistic legacy. With such a well-established commitment to the biggest and most incendiary issues of the day, with the talent, power, and standing to actually explore these issues in big-budget films that can be seen by millions of people, Streisand has, in the past fourteen years, opted to direct and/or act in only two films: the superficial *The Mirror Has Two Faces* and the silly *Meet the Fockers*. This dichotomy between the personally passionate and the professionally bland feature-film work adds up to nothing less than a total disconnect. If only . . .

What About Today?

. . . she is a pip to watch. Somewhat ill at ease in group scenes, in which she makes a doomed effort to fade into the scenery, she generates real warmth in her intimate exchanges with Mr. Stiller and especially Mr. Hoffman.

> —Manohla Dargis, *The New York Times,* December 22, 2004, on Barbra Streisand's performance in *Meet the Fockers*

If there's such a thing as hypoglycemic bliss in pop, it is to be found on *Guilty Pleasures.* . . . The lush, celestially oriented collection coproduced by Mr. Gibb with John Merchant is a sustained musical sugar rush. . . . But the question remains: What does this style and substance mean in 2005?

> —Stephen Holden, *The New York Times,* September 2005

Well, it wasn't exactly *The Normal Heart,* but after an eight-year absence, Barbra finally returned to the screen in 2004's *Meet the Fockers.* (It is worth noting that Streisand appears in films less frequently than almost any other major star in Hollywood history, having made eleven movies between 1968 and 1978, and a mere six additional films in the next twenty-six years.) By all accounts, marriage to James Brolin continued to relax Streisand, and her relative inactivity on the work front testifies to greater attention being paid to her personal life. Whatever the reason, the long absence guaranteed an avalanche of publicity when the film opened in December 2004, and the movie quickly became one of the fifty highest-grossing films of all time—the highest-grossing film of Barbra's career. The irony is that after the sheer professionalism of Streisand's own directorial vehicles, and the examination of thought-provoking ideas therein, whether successfully executed or not, this huge financial and popular success came in what is a ramshackle sketch of a film.

A sequel to 2001's *Meet the Parents, Meet the Fockers* continues the comic love match between male nurse Greg Focker (Ben Stiller) and his all-American fiancée, Pam Burns (Teri Polo). Now on the verge of marriage, Pam and Greg travel to Florida with Pam's parents: WASP matron Dina (Blythe Danner) and rigid, former CIA operative Jack (Robert De Niro). The object of the trip to Florida? A meeting with

ROS AND BERNIE FOCKER---2004'S WILDLY POPULAR *MEET THE FOCKERS*. *PHOTOFEST*

Greg's hippieish parents, Ros and Bernard Focker (Streisand and Dustin Hoffman). Needless to say, the inevitable culture clash ensues, right down to the film's fadeout at Greg and Pam's wedding.

In reality, the finished film's first, and only, inspired idea was the casting of Streisand and Hoffman as Greg's parents. These two stars make sense as a married couple onscreen; he loosens her up, and she, needless to say, does not disappear under his actorly schtick. It's Streisand and Hoffman who appear to be having the most fun on-screen, and there are, in fact, scattered moments of inspired silliness: the viewer's first glimpse of Barbra/Ros, a doctor, comes as she leads her sex therapy class for senior citizens (shades of *The Main Event,* albeit with Barbra leading a different kind of aerobics class; at least in *Fockers* the aerobics class is humorous). Tan, sporting a *Star Is Born* Afro-style hairdo, and wearing clothes and jewelry left over from the Woodstock years, Barbra as Ros appears to be having fun onscreen, as befits the author of a book entitled *Is Your Vagina Happy?* For his part,

Hoffman, playing a lawyer turned stay-at-home Dad, seems to relish scenes wherein his character shares much too much personal information: Upon meeting Pam's starchy parents, he thinks nothing of breaking the ice by discussing the fact that he has only one testicle and has had a vasectomy.

It's nice to see a relaxed Barbra back onscreen, but this is a role she can play with one hand tied behind her back, and there is nothing in the movie to stretch her prodigious talent in the slightest. Directed by Jay Roach, with a script by Jim Herzfeld and John Hamburg (and produced by De Niro, among others), *Meet the Fockers* lurches from one comic set piece to another, most of them a very long way from the wit of a *What's Up, Doc?*; not to mention a Billy Wilder film. Here the order of the day is Jinx the cat flushing Moses the dog down the toilet, De Niro sporting a fake breast in order to pacify his grandson Billy (De Niro's Jack calls the invention a "manary gland"), and toddler Billy learning his first word—*asshole*—from Greg.

There are only two facts of real note regarding Barbra Streisand's participartion in the film. First, Streisand is billed after Stiller, De Niro, and Hoffman, with the words *and Barbra Streisand*. Fourth billing? This would have been unthinkable even a few short years previously, and in fact the only other time in her film career when she received second billing was when she did so deliberately due to the extenuating circumstances of *All Night Long*. In *Meet the Fockers*, for the first time in her film career, Barbra Streisand plays neither the female lead nor the romantic interest—no small career sea change for a star of Streisand's magnitude.

Second, it is interesting to note that the scene of Ros giving a rough and tumble massage to Jack Burns (De Niro) was not in the original script and came about because Barbra requested that the scriptwriters provide a scene for her alone with De Niro. Whatever Barbra wants . . .

In the end, the disappointment a viewer might feel about Barbra's eight-year absence from the movies ending in a piece of nonsense like *Meet the Fockers* is really due to knowing Barbra's own high standards. *Fockers* proved sporadically funny, and certainly ended up a very big financial success, but because she has set the bar so high—raised such expectations because of her talent and infinite capacity for hard work—a successful trifle such as *Fockers* lingers in the memory as just that: a trifle.

On the recording front, a similar sense of anticipation greeted the release of Streisand's 2003 release: *The Movie Album*. After being remarkably silent creatively in the years following her marriage to James Brolin—no movies, compilation CDs only, and a mere four farewell concerts—Streisand released this long-awaited CD in the fall of 2003. In its own peculiar way, *The Movie Album* reflects everything right—and wrong—with Streisand's later career.

On the plus side, she sounds in very good voice, amazingly so for a sixty-one-year-old woman. Maybe a few top notes have been lost, but that's about it. The singing is rich—Richard Rodgers was right, there is the depth of a cello—and the performances are models of restraint. No sobs or hysterics, no, to use her own words, "*geshrey*ing." It's not the singing that is at fault, and critics were generally positive, with Stephen Holden in the *New York Times* calling it her finest recording since *The Broadway Album* eighteen years earlier. The CD garnered Streisand her thirty-eighth Grammy nomination (Best Traditional Pop Recording) and debuted at #5 on the pop charts—excellent for anyone, but extraordinary for a sixty-one-year-old singer of standards.

So what was the problem? In two words: the material. Clearly Streisand was in a mellow mood when recording the CD, but at this stage of her career, with seemingly no one willing to say no to her, the surfeit of ballads lent the disc a sameness. In an odd twist, critics generally seemed more pleased than fans, and although selling very well initially, the CD quickly dropped out of the top 100 after achieving gold status (her forty-ninth gold record—a record for female singers).

Simply put, it's great to hear one famous movie theme (e.g. "Smile") swathed in violins and a seventy-five-piece orchestra, but when followed by another ("Moon River") and another ("Wild Is the Wind") and yet another ("Emily"), the unthinkable for a Barbra Streisand CD happens: one stops listening. There is nothing compelling, nothing demanding one's attention. Barbra Streisand as musical wallpaper? Well, yes. Who'da thunk it?

A sense of sameness ruins the effectiveness of the CD, but fortunately the CD contains only one outright clunker: "More in Love with You" from *The 4 Horsemen of the Apocalypse,* a musical theme by André Previn that Streisand loved so much she walked down the aisle to it on her wedding day. Outfitted with a new specially created chamber music arrangement for the wedding day by that fellow, what's his name—oh yes, Marvin Hamlisch, the song also gained a new lyric by the Bergmans, which was decidedly one of their lesser efforts.

However, the Bergmans are better represented on the CD by Streisand's definitive interpretation of "How Do You Keep the Music Playing." A lovely, flowing melody by Michel Legrand complements their knowing, bittersweet lyrics, and Streisand invests it with an entirely appropriate sense of urgency and emotion. Oh, the drama of it all.

> *The more I love, the more that I'm afraid*
> *That in your eyes, I may not see*
> *Forever . . . Forever.*

These lyrics represent a larger-than-life Hollywood kind of love, the forever and ever, "Don't let's ask for the moon when we have the stars" kind of onscreen love to which young Barbra Joan responded so intensely. You can take the girl out of the Lowe's King movie theater in Brooklyn, but you can't . . .

What made *The Broadway Album* brilliant was not just the extraordinary selection of songs, led by Streisand's exploration of the Sondheim canon. It was the pacing of the album, pacing that touched on the well-known themes of Streisand's life. Statement of theme— "Putting It Together"; yearning romantic ballad—"If I Loved You"; urgency about life's possibilities—"Something's Coming." By contrast, on *The Movie Album* the sameness of song selection and arrangements becomes aural mush, relieved only by a lovely lilting bossa-nova rendition of "I'm in the Mood for Love" and the closer: the all-stops-out Broadway-style belter "You're Gonna Hear From Me."

A very different note was struck by Barbra's most recent CD, 2005's *Guilty Pleasures*. When the news began to circulate that Barbra and Barry Gibb would reunite to record a new CD, much was made of the fact that the recording would be released in September 2005 to coincide with the twenty-fifth anniversary of *Guilty*'s original release. And, in a nutshell, therein lies the rub. When *Guilty* was released in 1980, the trademark Gibbs/BeeGees sound was still riding the wave of popularity that had peaked with 1978's *Saturday Night Fever*. In 2005, the BeeGees' reign on the charts long over, the release of *Guilty Pleasures* leaves one wondering only one thing: Exactly why did Barbra Streisand record any of these songs?

This technicolor Streisand/Gibb collaboration echoes its predecessor right down the line; in fact, lest any marketing opportunity be missed, its release was even preceded by a reissue of *Guilty,* a reissue that listed many "new" extras, all of which boiled down to some leftover 1980 still photographs and a preview of the new CD. The similarities between the two recordings begins with the monochromatic design of the packaging: *Guilty* was drenched in white, while *Guilty Pleasures* finds the duo dressed in black, posing against a back-lit black background. *Guilty* had two duets—the title song and "What Kind of Fool"—and *Guilty Pleasures* has two duets—"Come Tomorrow" and "Above the Law." Barry Gibb wrote the majority of the songs on *Guilty* with his brothers Robin and Maurice; on *Guilty Pleasures* he wrote nearly all of the songs with his sons Ashley and Stephen. In short, all of the proper and parallel bases were touched; the problem was that the end result was rarely inspired.

It's not that the CD is bad—it's actually pleasant, forgettable pop fluff and sold fairly well. Debuting at number five on the charts (Streisand's twenty-eighth top-ten album), the disc became her fiftieth gold record within five weeks of its release. The CD/DVD dual disc is professional to its core, both visually (credits include key hair, key makeup, and lighting consulting by no less than esteemed cinematographer Laszlo Kovacks) and, of course, musically. Gibb, a talented pop craftsman, cushions the Streisand vocals on his trademark layers of sound, floating Barbra's voice on clouds of support. And that is exactly where the problem begins.

Even after repeated listenings to the CD, one easily remembers the BeeGees–style production and backing harmonies but very little of the Streisand vocals. At her best, like any original artist, Barbra Streisand transforms material, investing multilayered music and lyrics (e.g., Sondheim and Arlen) with all of her considerable passion and driving intelligence. When presented with meaningless fluff, the Streisand voice either overwhelms the material or, as is the case here, disappears, literally and figuratively. On "It's Up to You," the CD's fourth cut, her voice is completely overpowered by the music. The very next cut, "Night of My Life," is filled with thumping drums and guitar lines that recall the disco era, but tell us nothing about the vocalist. What is Barbra Streisand even singing about here? On "Without Your Love," Barbra/Barry tell us "Your dark became my night"—huh? This lyric is followed a few lines later by "There were diamonds in the dust." What? Where? On "All the Children," we are informed no fewer than eight times that "All the children will dance and sing for you." Not exactly providing insight into the human condition, these lyrics at times dissolve into murmured sweet nothings that are so inconsequential as to make the songs on *Guilty* sound like a combination of Sondheim and Brecht.

If the lyrics consistently disappoint, the music is oftentimes quite fun. The opening cut of "Come Tomorrow" features sax work by Tom Scott (who figured so prominently on *Butterfly*) that echoes early rock 'n' roll and even injects a bit of rhythm and blues into the proceedings. The first single, "Stranger in a Strange Land," accompanied on the DVD by a video in support of troops, is a catchy melody strangely reminiscent of the Gershwins' "Strike Up the Band." "Above the Law" demonstrates how the Streisand and Gibb voices can blend together so effectively, and with its climbing counterpoint harmonies, pleasantly echoes *Guilty*'s "What Kind of Fool." There is even a fun remake of Andy Gibb's "Don't Throw It All Away" that presents Barbra with one of her few opportunities to occasionally let loose with her trademark soaring vocals.

The CD ends, appropriately enough, with "Letting Go" (written by Barry Gibb more than twenty years previously). It is the one cut on the CD wherein Barbra's voice is out front, unadorned and often accompanied only by piano. One notes in passing the slight breath control problems heard on the more extended vocal lines, but generally speaking, the voice is in very good shape. On this cut, Barbra's voice, and not the production's trademark BeeGees sound, is telling the story. The problem is that when the CD is viewed in overall terms, these first-rate moments are outnumbered by meandering tracks that resemble nothing so much as a marketing concept in search of an album.

If, then, *Guilty Pleasures* remains at best a semi-pleasant diversion, the vocal equivalent of 2004's equally disposable *Meet the Fockers,* the true Streisand vocal legacy is best summed up by the final track on 2003's *The Movie Album,* "You're Gonna Hear from Me." This closing song reminds everyone why, forty years on, the listener is still riveted. It's all there: the driving ambition, the need to be noticed, a will of steel, and above all, THAT VOICE, soaring over a full orchestra.

In the liner notes, Streisand writes, " 'You're Gonna Hear from

Me' reminded me of some of the songs from the early days of my career." Hell, no. It's not the songs that one is reminded of. It's the eighteen-year-old Barbra Joan Streisand herself. The ferocious ambition with the talent and drive to back it up—that's what resonates with this song.

Her voice gaining in intensity as the music surges, Streisand definitely knows her way around these Dory Previn lyrics:

> *Make me some room, you people up there*
> *On top of the world, I'll meet you I swear*
> *I'm staking my claim, remember my name!*
> *You're gonna hear from me*

Sixty-one years old and still running at full speed. Belting it out for anyone who needed to leave their hick town, move to New York City or Hollywood, and be noticed. "Understand me. Watch me. Like it or not, you have no choice." Which is the only way Barbra—and her fans—would have it.

Career Scorecard

YEAR	WORK	GRADE	COMMENT
1962	. . . WHOLESALE NY Drama Critics Best Supporting Actress (tie) Tony Award Nomination—Best Supporting Actress	B	Barbra as Broadway baby
1962	. . . WHOLESALE— cast album	B	"Miss Marmelstein" preserved on disc
1963	PINS AND NEEDLES— album	B	Five songs
1963	THE BARBRA STREISAND ALBUM Gold Record Grammy Award— Album of the Year Grammy Award— Best Vocal Performance—Female Grammy Nomination— "Happy Days Are Here Again"	B	Exciting but uneven
1963	THE SECOND BARBRA STREISAND ALBUM Gold Record	A	First class

YEAR	WORK	GRADE	COMMENT
1963	GUEST APPEARANCE— JUDY GARLAND TELEVISION SERIES Emmy Nomination— Outstanding Performance in Variety or Music Program	A	A meeting of legends
1964	THE THIRD ALBUM Gold Record	A	Extraordinary
1964	FUNNY GIRL— Broadway Tony Nomination— Best Actress in a Musical	A	Queen of Broadway—with good reason
1964	FUNNY GIRL— cast album Gold Record	A	Quintessential cast recording—great
1965	PEOPLE—album Gold, Platinum Records Grammy Award— Best Vocal Performance—Female Grammy Nomination— Album of the Year Grammy Nomination— Record of the Year— "People"	A	Nary a false step
1965	MY NAME IS BARBRA— television special Emmy Award— Outstanding Program Achievement Emmy Award— Outstanding Individual Achievement	A	Queen of television
1965	MY NAME IS BARBRA— record album Grammy Award— Best Vocal Performance—Female Grammy Award Nomination— Album of the Year	A	Great singing

YEAR	WORK	GRADE	COMMENT
1965	MY NAME IS BARBRA, TWO . . . Gold, Platinum Records	A	First-rate vocals
1966	COLOR ME BARBRA— television special	A	Barbra in color; every bit as good as *My Name Is Barbra*
1966	COLOR ME BARBRA— record album Gold Record	A	Firing on all cylinders
1966	HAROLD SINGS ARLEN (WITH FRIEND)	B	Loyalty to her early champion
1966	JE M'APPELLE BARBRA Gold Record	A	Excellent
1967	SIMPLY STREISAND Gold Record	A	Every track a winner; one of her two best recordings
1967	BELLE OF 14TH STREET— television special	D	Awful
1967	A CHRISTMAS ALBUM Grammy Nomination— Best Contemporary Pop Album Gold, Platinum × 5	A	Great singing, great song choices
1968	A HAPPENING IN CENTRAL PARK— television special Emmy Nomination— Outstanding Variety or Musical Production	B	Fun
1968	A HAPPENING IN CENTRAL PARK— record album	B	Good and safe
1968	FUNNY GIRL—film Academy Award— Best Actress	A	New queen of Hollywood— deservedly so

YEAR	WORK	GRADE	COMMENT
	Golden Globe Award— Best Actress Musical or Comedy		
1968	FUNNY GIRL— soundtrack Gold, Platinum Records	A	Singing even better than on the cast album
1969	WHAT ABOUT TODAY	C	Confused and confusing
1969	HELLO, DOLLY— film Golden Globe Nomination— Best Actress— Musical or Comedy	B	Better than Barbra thinks it is
1969	HELLO, DOLLY— soundtrack	B	Old-fashioned in the good sense of the phrase
1969	ASCAP Pied Piper Award		
1969	GREATEST HITS Gold, Platinum × 2	B	Decent compilation, but not all cuts were even hits
1970	ON A CLEAR DAY . . . —film	B	Great in the nineteenth century, not in the twentieth
1970	ON A CLEAR DAY . . . —soundtrack	B	Nice score; first rate Riddle arrangements
1970	THE OWL AND THE PUSSYCAT— film Golden Globe Nomination— Best Actress— Musical or Comedy	B	First nonmusical film; freewheeling and ribald performance
1970	THE OWL AND THE PUSSYCAT— soundtrack	B	Dialogue from the film—crass and funny

YEAR	WORK	GRADE	COMMENT
1970	Tony Award— Star of the Decade		
1970	Golden Globe Award— World Film Favorite		
1971	Golden Globe Award— World Film Favorite		
1971	STONEY END Gold, Platinum Records	B	Best of the "rock" efforts
1971	BARBRA JOAN STREISAND Gold Record	C	So-so, but the Bacharach medley is a classic
1972	CONCERT AT THE FORUM Gold, Platinum Records Grammy nomination— Best Pop Vocal Performance, "Sweet Inspiration/ Where You Lead"	B	Good, but the later concerts are much better
1972	WHAT'S UP, DOC?	A	Terrific comic performance; never more relaxed onscreen
1972	UP THE SANDBOX	C	Valiant effort, but a real *tsimmis*
1973	BARBRA STREISAND AND OTHER MUSICAL INSTRUMENTS— television special Emmy Nomination— Outstanding Comedy, Variety, or Musical Special	D	Misfire
	BARBRA STREISAND AND OTHER MUSICAL INSTRUMENTS— soundtrack	D	Unappealing

YEAR	WORK	GRADE	COMMENT
1973	THE WAY WE WERE—film Academy Award Nomination—Best Actress Golden Globe Nomination—Best Actress—Motion Picture Drama	A	Excellent acting job; a wallow for fans
1974	THE WAY WE WERE—soundtrack Gold Record	B	A real movie-movie score, plus the hit title song
1974	THE WAY WE WERE—vocal album Gold, Platinum × 2	B	Surprisingly effective melding of genres
1974	FOR PETE'S SAKE—film	D	Waste of time—Barbra's and the audience's
1974	BUTTERFLY—album Gold Record	C	Tries too hard to be hip
1975	FUNNY LADY—film Golden Globe Nomination—Best Actress—Musical or Comedy	B	Up and down
	FUNNY LADY—soundtrack Gold Record	B	Nice score—in great voice
1975	Golden Globe Award—World Film Favorite		
1975	LAZY AFTERNOON—album Gold Record	B	One of her better contemporary pop albums
1976	CLASSICAL BARBRA—album Gold Record	C	Overly reverential

YEAR	WORK	GRADE	COMMENT
	Grammy nomination— Best Classical Vocal Soloist Performance		
1976	A STAR IS BORN— film Academy Award— Best Song— "Evergreen" (composer) Golden Globe— Best Motion Picture—Musical or Comedy Golden Globe— Best Motion Picture Actress— Musical or Comedy Golden Globe— Best Song— "Evergreen" (composer)	D	Worse than Barbra thinks it is
	A STAR IS BORN— soundtrack Gold, Platinum × 4 Grammy Award— "Evergreen"— Song of the Year (composer) Grammy Award— "Evergreen"— Best Pop Vocal Performance—Female Grammy Nomination— "Evergreen"— Record of the Year Grammy Nomination— "A Star Is Born"— Best Original Score	C	Three good songs; forget the rest
1977	STREISAND SUPERMAN— album Gold, Platinum × 2	C	Okay, nothing more

YEAR	WORK	GRADE	COMMENT
1978	SONGBIRD—album Gold, Platinum Records Grammy Nomination— "You Don't Bring Me Flowers," Pop Vocal Female—Solo	C	Fairly forgettable
1978	GREATEST HITS VOLUME 2—album Gold, Platinum × 5 Grammy Nomination— "You Don't Bring Me Flowers," duet with Neil Diamond	B	Good songs, but we've heard it all before
1978	Golden Globe Award—World Film Favorite		
1979	THE MAIN EVENT— film	D	Awful
	THE MAIN EVENT— soundtrack	D	Filler music, plus one vocal, the generic disco title song
1979	WET—album Gold, Platinum Records	C	Concept goes nowhere
1980	GUILTY—album Gold, Platinum × 5 Grammy Award— "Guilty"—Best Pop Vocal Performance by Duo or Group— with Barry Gibb Grammy nomination— Album of the Year Grammy nomination— Record of the Year— "Woman in Love" Grammy nomination— Best Pop Female Vocal Performance— "Woman in Love"	A	Great; best of her contemporary pop albums

YEAR	WORK	GRADE	COMMENT
1981	ALL NIGHT LONG— film	D	Why?
1981	MEMORIES—album Gold, Platinum × 5	C	Basically a compilation— again
1983	YENTL—film Golden Globe Award—Best Motion Picture— Musical or Comedy Golden Globe Award—Best Director Golden Globe Nomination— Best Actress— Musical or Comedy	A	A first-rate film; great directorial debut
	YENTL—soundtrack Gold, Platinum Records	B	Very good Legrand/Bergmans score
1984	EMOTION—album Gold, Platinum Records	F	Totally unnecessary and forgettable
1985	THE BROADWAY ALBUM Gold, Platinum × 4 Grammy Award— Best Pop Female Vocal Grammy Nomination— Album of the Year	A	As good as it gets; her best album
1986	ONE VOICE— television special	B	Nice work
	ONE VOICE—CD Grammy Nomination— Best Pop Female Vocal Performance	B	In good voice; basically old material with three great new cuts

YEAR	WORK	GRADE	COMMENT
1987	NUTS–film Golden Globe Nomination—Best Actress in Motion Picture—Drama	B	Better than the critics admitted
1987	NUTS—soundtrack (composer)	B	Fairly effective
1988	TILL I LOVED YOU— CD Gold, Platinum Records	C	Bland song cycle
1989	A COLLECTION . . . GREATEST HITS AND MORE—CD Gold, Platinum × 2	B	Basically a compilation—again
1991	THE PRINCE OF TIDES—film Academy Award Nomination—Best Picture (as producer) Directors Guild of America Nomination— Best Director Golden Globe Nomination—Best Director Motion Picture—Drama	B	Great directing
	THE PRINCE OF TIDES—soundtrack	A	Terrific James Newton Howard score and two first-rate vocals
1991	JUST FOR THE RECORD Gold, Platinum Records Grammy Nomination— Best Traditional Pop Vocal Performance— "Warm All Over"	A	Excellent, fascinating boxed set
1992	Grammy Legend Award		

YEAR	WORK	GRADE	COMMENT
1993	BACK TO BROADWAY Gold, Platinum × 2 Grammy Nomination— Best Traditional Pop Vocal Performance Grammy Nomination— Best Pop Vocal Performance— Duo or Group— "Music of the Night"	B	Very good—just not as good as *The Broadway Album*
1994	THE CONCERT—CD Gold, Platinum × 3 Grammy Nomination— Traditional Pop Vocal Performance— "The Concert" CD Grammy Nomination— Best Pop Vocal Performance—Female— "Ordinary Miracles"	A	Career peak
1994	THE CONCERT— television special Emmy Award— Outstanding Variety Music or Comedy Special Emmy Award— Outstanding Individual Performance in a Variety or Music Program Directors Guild of America—Outstanding Directorial Achievement in Musical/Variety Television Program	A	Career peak
1995	Cable ACE Award— Best Performance in Music Special or Series Cable ACE Award— Best Direction of a Music Special or Series Peabody Award		

YEAR	WORK	GRADE	COMMENT
1995	Grammy Lifetime Achievement Award		
1995	SERVING IN SILENCE Emmy Award Nomination— Producer—Outstanding Made-for-Television Movie	B	First-rate television movie
1996	THE MIRROR HAS TWO FACES—film Academy Award Nomination—Best Song Composer— "I Finally Found Someone" Golden Globe Nomination—Best Original Song Composer Golden Globe Nomination— Best Actress— Musical or Comedy	C	Unnecessary— rehashing old personal issues
	THE MIRROR HAS TWO FACES— soundtrack Gold, Platinum Records Grammy nomination— Best Pop Collaboration with Vocals—"I Finally Found Someone," with Bryan Adams	C	Score and two vocals; of no particlar note
1997	HIGHER GROUND—CD Gold, Platinum × 3 Grammy Nomination— Best Pop Vocal Duo—"Tell Him," with Celine Dion	C	Great idea, uninspired song selection
1999	A LOVE LIKE OURS— CD	C	Nice idea, but the songs are mostly

YEAR	WORK	GRADE	COMMENT
	Gold, Platinum Records		greeting-card mush
2000	TIMELESS—CD Gold, Platinum Records Grammy Nomination— Best Traditional Pop Vocal Album	B	Live career retrospective; touches all bases
	TIMELESS— television special Emmy Award— Outstanding Individual Performance in Variety or Music Program	B	Nice Directing
2000	REEL MODELS: THE FIRST WOMEN OF FILM—AMC Produced by Barwood Films; Executive Producer Barbra Streisand Documentary introduced by Streisand Daytime Emmy Award—Outstanding Special Class Special	B	Interesting film history
2000	THE LIVING CENTURY— PBS—Executive Producer Barbra Streisand	A	Excellent documentary of centenarians
2000	Golden Globe Award— Cecil B. DeMille Lifetime Achievement Award		
2001	CHRISTMAS MEMORIES— CD Grammy Nomination— Best Traditional Pop Vocal Album	A	First rate; great pop singing and terrific song selection
2001	American Film Institute Life Achievement Award		

YEAR	WORK	GRADE	COMMENT
2002	ESSENTIAL BARBRA STREISAND—CD Gold, Platinum Records	B	A compilation—again
2002	DUETS—CD Gold Record	C	A compilation—again
2003	THE MOVIE ALBUM—CD Gold, Platinum Records Grammy Nomination—Best Traditional Pop Vocal Album	C	Great idea but a surfeit of ballads
2004	MEET THE FOCKERS—film	C	Nice to See Babs onscreen again, but an eight-year wait for this?
2005	GUILTY PLEASURES—CD Gold Record	C	Pleasant but disposable pop fluff

All-time best-selling
pop music
female vocalist
50 gold records—
second only to
Elvis Presley
13 multi-platinum
albums
31 platinum albums

Note: Cameo recordings
(e.g., soundtrack of
EYES OF LAURA MARS)
are not included in
this appendix, nor are
45 r.p.m. singles.
Guest-star television
appearances are not
included, with the exception
of THE JUDY GARLAND SHOW
appearance

Notes

PREFACE

"The professional is the guy": Hamill, Pete, *Why Sinatra Matters,* New York: Little Brown & Company, 1998, p. 18

"Putting it Together," from the Broadway musical *Sunday in the Park with George,* music and lyrics by Stephen Sondheim.

"Her work is exactly": program notes, *Barbra Streisand—Timeless—Live in Concert,* p. 12

BEGINNINGS

"She has made life": Isobel Lennart as quoted by Ira Mothner, "Barbra," *Look,* October 15, 1968

"I'm Still Here": from the Broadway musical *Follies,* music and lyrics by Stephen Sondheim

"When the rabbi": "Superbarbra" by Thomas Morgan, *Look,* April 5, 1966

"Through the years": *US,* October 9, 2000

"T-Strap shoes": Edwards, Anne, *Streisand: A Biography,* New York: Little Brown, 1997, p. 94

"At the Bon Soir": Gavin, James, *Intimate Nights,* New York: Limelight

Editions, 1992; also quoted in Kevin Sessums, "Streisand Now," *Vanity Fair,* November 1991

"She asked instead": *Ibid.,* p. 106

"Totally embarrassed by me": Kevin Sessums, *Op. Cit.*

"Get a swelled head": Bernard Weinraub, "Barbra Streisand Still Not Pretty Enough," *The New York Times,* November 13, 1996

"When I was 18": *Ibid.*

"Yeah, you did good": Edwards, *Op. Cit.,* p. 106

"This comment was poignantly echoed": "A Star Is Reborn," Michael Shnayerson, *Vanity Fair,* November 1994

"Get along better now": *Ibid.*

"But by her not understanding me": Sessums, *Op. Cit.*

"(My mother) said she didn't want me": Weinraub, *Op. Cit.*

RECORDINGS

"Streisand is tempermental": Friedwald, Will, *Sinatra! The Song Is You,* New York: Scribner, 1995, p. 34

"When she sings the medley": Stephen Holden, *Rolling Stone,* Issue 99, 1971

"Frank Sinatra fan letter": Shana Alexander, *LIFE,* May 22, 1964

"The Way We Were": Marvin Hamlisch, Alan & Marilyn Bergman (Colgems–EMI Music Inc./ASCAP)

"Upon their first meeting": *Woman,* November 5, 1978

"Guava Jelly": words and music by Bob Marley

"Pretend to share their star power": Jon Pareles, *The New York Times,* June 22, 1994

"Evergreen," from the motion picture *A Star Is Born,* music by Barbra Streisand, lyrics by Paul Williams

"Niagara": by Marvin Hamlisch, C. Bayer Sager, and B. Roberts

"Guilty": by Barry Gibb, Robin Gibb, Maurice Gibb

"Swooping melodies": Barbra Streisand, "Just for the Record," Columbia Records, Sony Music Entertainment, Inc., booklet, p. 52

"I made *Yentl*": Jack Neufield, "Diva Democracy," *George,* November 1996

". . . just cringed listening to": Barbra Streisand, interview with Stephen Holden, *The New York Times,* November 10, 1985

"Putting It Together" from the Broadway musical *Sunday in the Park with George,* music and lyrics by Stephen Sondheim

"Sondheim and Streisand worked on": Zadan, Craig, *Sondheim & Company,* New York: Harper and Row, 1974, 2nd Edition, 1986, p. 290

"Here the singer and the song": Alan and Marilyn Bergman, liner notes, *The Broadway Album,* Columbia Records, Sony Music Entertainment Inc., 1985

"For some time I had dreamed": Barbra Streisand, "Just for the Record," Columbia Records, Sony Music Entertainment, Inc., booklet, p. 83

"For All We Know": by J. Fred Coots, S. M. Lewis

"I'm so far out": *PM East,* Group W Television, Appearances October 1961–January 1962

"You're the Top": music and lyrics by Cole Porter

"Can You Tell the Moment": music by Michel Legrand, lyrics by Alan & Marilyn Bergman

"Move On": from the Broadway musical *Sunday in the Park with George,* music and lyrics by Stephen Sondheim

"greater richness, clarity": Jay Landers, liner notes for *Christmas Memories,* Columbia Records, Sony Music Entertainment, Inc., 2001

"A House Is Not a Home": music by Burt Bacharach, lyrics by Hal David

FILMS

"This reputation about being difficult": Sessums, *Op. Cit.*

"Don't Rain on My Parade," from the Broadway musical *Funny Girl,* music by Jule Styne, lyrics by Bob Merrill

"My Man," Maurice Yvain/Channing Pollock/Albert Willemetz/ Jacques Charles

"Plain brown wrapper," *The Owl and the Pussycat,* screenplay by Buck Henry based on the play by Bill Manhoff, Columbia Pictures/Rastar, 1970

"For whom do you model," *Ibid.*

"Makes her lines funny musically": Pauline Kael, *The New Yorker,* November 14, 1970

"Close to Charles A. Stephens's": Vincent Canby, *The New York Times,* November 4, 1970

"What would my mother think," Riese, Randall: *Her Name is Barbra,* New York: Birch Lane Press, 1993, pp. 310–311

"Joyful mess," Pauline Kael, *The New Yorker,* December 30, 1972

"Like the country he lived in": *The Way We Were,* screenplay by Arthur Laurents, Columbia Pictures Industries Inc./Rastar, 1973

"She has become an establishment": Herb Ross, *The Movie Star Book,* New York: Workman Publishing Company, Inc., Danny Peary Editor, 1978

"losing illusions": *Newsweek,* 1975

"They're gonna build me": *Funny Lady,* screenplay by Jay Presson Allen, Arnold Schulman, story by Arnold Schulman, Columbia/Rastar/Persky-Bright/Vista 1975

"How Lucky Can You Get": from the motion picture *Funny Lady,* music by John Kander, lyrics by Fred Ebb

"Will there be": Molly Haskell, *The Village Voice,* March 24, 1975

"You can see the movie makers": Pauline Kael, *The New Yorker,* March 17, 1975

"Barbara sings to make you forget": Frank Pierson, *New West,* November 22, 1976

"I'll be your groupie": *A Star Is Born,* screenplay by Joan Didion & John Gregory Dunne and Frank Pierson based on the original story by William Wellman and Robert Carson, Warner Brothers/First Artists, 1976

"I'm sorry girls": *Ibid.*

"Evergreen": from the motion picture *A Star Is Born,* music by Barbra Streisand, lyrics by Paul Williams

"Introduced by Jane Fonda": Academy Awards Oscar's Greatest Moments 1971–1991

"Great ass": *Woman,* November 5, 1978

"You make me feel cheap": *The Main Event,* screenplay by Gail Parent and Andrew Smith, Warner Brothers/First Artists/Barwood, 1979

"You're having an affair with": *All Night Long,* screenplay by W.D. Richter, Universal 1981

"Story books for women": *Yentl,* screenplay by Jack Rosenthal, Barbra Streisand, story Isaac Bashevis Singer, MGM/UA 1983

"Piece of Sky": from the motion picture *Yentl,* music by Michel Legrand, lyrics by Alan and Marilyn Bergman

"It is said that": Edwards, *Op. Cit.,* Miller, Gabriel, *The Films of Martin Ritt, Fanfare for the Common Man,* Jackson: University Press of Mississippi, 2000

"Ritt felt that" Edwards, *Op. Cit.,* Miller, *Op. Cit.*

"You know what I use": *Nuts,* screenplay by Tom Topor, Darryl Ponsican, Alvin Sargent, based upon the play by Tom Topor, Warner Brothers, 1987

"Forgiving her own mother": Sessums, *Op. Cit.*

"When I was faced with the potential loss of my mother": *Ibid.*

"And when Kramer publicly attacked her": *Variety,* April 8, 1996

"I never should have encouraged you to speak": *The Mirror Has Two Faces,* story and screenplay by Richard LaGravenese, TriStar Pictures in association with Phoenix Pictures, 1996

"You're a very sick man": *Ibid.*

"I took every precaution": *Ibid.*

"What did you want to say?": *Ibid.*

"I don't care if you're pretty": *Ibid.*

TELEVISION

"I scare you, don't I?" *PM East,* Group W Television, appearances October 1961–January 1962, private tapes

"Can we just start the interview": *60 Minutes,* November 24, 1991

"Who wouldn't be proud?" *Ibid.*

"You don't do enough singing": *Ibid.*

"Thirty years ago I didn't like you": *Ibid.*

"Well if I really am your guest": *The Judy Garland Show,* CBS Television, Broadcast October 6, 1963, DVD Volume 5

"Starting Here Starting Now," David Shire–Richard Maltby Jr.

"I think it's enormous": *One Voice,* HBO Television, filmed September 6, 1986, broadcast December 27, 1986

"I've never seen her live": *Ibid.*

"Somewhere": from the Broadway musical *West Side Story,* music by Leonard Bernstein, lyrics by Stephen Sondheim

CONCERTS

"One million calls": Edwards, *Op. Cit.,* p. 486.

"Streisand's assets were": Tom Shales, *The Washington Post,* December 15, 1991

"According to the *New York Times*": William Grimes, *The New York Times,* April 3, 1994

"Lost in all of the": Shnayerson, *Op. Cit.*

"As If We Never Said Goodbye": from the musical *Sunset Boulevard,* by Andrew Lloyd Webber, Don Black, Christopher Hampton, and Amy Powers

"As Jon Pareles pointed out": "Local Girl Makes Good, Sings," *The New York Times,* June 22, 1994

"On a Clear Day You Can See Forever," from the Broadway musical *On a Clear Day You Can See Forever,* music by Burton Lane, lyrics by Alan Jay Lerner

"A Piece of Sky": from the motion picture *Yentl,* MGM/UA, 1983, music by Michel Legrand, lyrics by Alan and Marilyn Bergman

"For All We Know" by J. Fred Coots-S.M. Lewis.

"My idea of a perfect world": "The Concert," Columbia Records/Sony Music Entertainment Inc., 1994

"Somewhere": from the Broadway musical *West Side Story,* music by Leonard Bernstein, lyrics by Stephen Sondheim

"New York is my home": *US,* October 9, 2000

"This time around": *US,* October 9, 2000

THEATER

"There is only one way": *Vanity Fair,* November, 1991, Kevin Sessums, "Streisand Now"

"Was there a mobile secretary's chair onstage?": *Original Story By,* Laurents, Arthur: New York: Knopf, 2000, p. 222

"Take-ums": *Ibid.*

For information regarding the production period for *Funny Girl* on Broadway, reference was made to the following sources: *Streisand— The Woman and the Legend* by James Spada, New York: Doubleday, 1981, pp. 62–70; Edwards, Anne, *Op. Cit.,* pp. 162–199; reissue of *Funny Girl* original cast recording copyright 1964 Capitol Records, reissue CD on Angel Records, 1992, EMI, liner notes by David Foil.

"Ego crushing experience": Isobel Lennart as quoted in *Look,* October 15, 1968

"She carries her own spotlight": Jule Styne as quoted by Ray Kennedy in *Time* magazine, April 10, 1964

"Don't Rain on My Parade," from the Broadway musical *Funny Girl,* music by Jule Styne, lyrics by Bob Merrill

"She performs the daunting feat": Herbert Kretzmer, *London Express,* April 19, 1966

"Rose's Turn," from the Broadway musical *Gypsy,* music by Jule Styne, lyrics by Stephen Sondheim

POLITICS

"I'm a feminist": Jack Neufield, *Op. Cit.*

"Tikkun olam": *Ibid.*

"Fabrent": Sessums, *Op. Cit.*

"I feel like I am my father's daughter": Neufield, *Op. Cit.*

". . . helped ensure that Roe v. Wade": *Ibid.*

"Distributed money to anti-choice Democrats": *Ibid.*

"A man is a perfectionist": Barbra Streisand, Women in Film's 1992 Crystal Awards Lunch, as quoted in *Premiere,* Special Issue 1993

"And I look forward to a society": *Ibid.*

"Genocidal denial": Barbra Streisand, 1992, "Commitment to Life VI," AIDS Project L.A.

"What the hell is Alan Greenspan": Shnayerson, *Op. Cit.*

"I don't want to go around": Neufield, *Op. Cit.*

"I don't want to give the impression": *Ibid.*

"Waging a war for the soul of America": Barbra Streisand, "The Artist as Citizen," speech given at Harvard University, February 3, 1995

"Is this a new McCarthyism": *Ibid.*

"Alfie," from the motion picture *Alfie,* music by Burt Bacharach, lyrics by Hal David.

"You're a doll": White House Press Correspondents Dinner, May 17,

1963, as reported by Ray Kennedy in *Time,* April 10, 1964

"I think we should send Barbra to Washington": Barry Manilow, concert fundraiser for Democratic Congress Campaign Committee,
September 29, 2002, as reported in *The New York Times,* September
30, 2002

"Paralyzed, demoralized, depressed": *The New York Times,* April 10,
2001

"It's time for the Democrats": *The New York Times,* September 30, 2002

"Multi-million dollar tax deduction": Edwards, *Op. Cit.,* p. 489

"She is simply not afraid of the criticism": Shnayerson, *Op. Cit.*

WHAT ABOUT TODAY?

"Second it is interesting to note": "Boldface" by Joyce Wadler, *The
New York Times,* December 21, 2004

"Geshreying": *Playboy,* October 1977

"More in Love with You," from the motion picture *The 4 Horsemen of
the Apocalypse,* music by André Previn, lyrics by Alan and Marilyn
Bergman

"How Do You Keep the Music Playing," from the motion picture
Best Friends, music by Michel Legrand, lyrics by Alan and Marilyn
Bergman

"Without Your Love," written by Barry Gibb and Ashley Gibb, 2005,
Crompton Songs (BMI)

"All the Children," written by Barry Gibb, Ashley Gibb, and Stephen
Gibb, 2005, Crompton Songs (BMI)

" 'You're Gonna Hear from Me' reminded me": Barbra Streisand, liner
notes, *The Movie Album,* Columbia Records, Sony Music Entertainment Inc. 2003

"You're Gonna Hear from Me," from the motion picture *Inside Daisy
Clover,* music by André Previn, lyrics by Dory Previn

Bibliography

Basinger, Jeanine, *The Films of Gene Kelly.* New York: Pyramid Communications, 1976

Considine, Shaun, *Barbra Streisand: The Woman, the Myth, the Music.* New York: Delacorte Press, 1985

Dunne, John Gregory. *Studio,* New York: Farrar, Straus & Giroux, 1969

Edwards, Anne. *Streisand: A Biography,* New York: Little Brown, 1997

Friedwald, Will. *Sinatra! The Song Is You: A Singer's Art.* New York: Scribner, 1995

Gavin, James. *Intimate Nights.* New York: Limelight Editions, 1992

Gottfried, Martin. *Broadway Musicals.* New York: Abradale Press/Harry N. Abrams, Inc. 1979, 1984

Grifin, Nancy and Masters, Kim. *Hit & Run: How Jon Peters and Peter Guber Took Sony for a Ride in Hollywood.* New York: Simon & Schuster, 1996

Hamill, Pete. *Why Sinatra Matters.* New York: Little Brown, 1998

Jordan, Rene. *The Greatest Star.* New York: Harper & Row, 1975

Kael, Pauline. *For Keeps: 30 Years at the Movies.* New York: Dutton, 1994

Katz, Ephraim. *The Film Encyclopedia.* New York: Putnam Publishing Group, 1979

Kissel, Howard. *The Abominable Showman*. New York: Applause Books, 1993

Laurents, Arthur. *Original Story By*. New York: Knopf, 2000

Miller, Gabriel, *The Films of Martin Ritt, Fanfare for the Common Man,* Jackson: University Press of Mississippi, 2000

Peary, Danny (ed.) *Close-Ups: The Movie Star Book*. New York: Workman Publishing Company, 1978

Riese, Randall. *Her Name Is Barbra*. New York: Birch Lane Press, 1993

Secrest, Meryl. *Stephen Sondheim: A Life*. London: Bloomsbury Publishing Plc, 1998

Sennett, Ted. *Hollywood Musicals*. New York: Harry N. Abrams Inc. 1981

Spada, James. *The First Decade—The Films and Career of Barbra Streisand*. New York: Citadel Press, 1974

————. *The Woman and the Legend*. New York: Doubleday, 1981

Thomson, David. *A Biographical Dictionary of Film*. New York: William Morrow and Company, Inc., 1976

Torme, Mel. *Judy Garland: The Other Side of the Rainbow*. New York: Morrow 1970

Zadan, Craig. *Sondheim & Co.,* New York: Harper & Row, 1974, second edition-1986

ARCHIVES

The Billy Rose Theatre Collection, Lincoln Center Library for the Performing Arts

New York City Museum of Television and Radio, New York City

MAGAZINES, PERIODICALS, AND NEWSPAPERS

George: November 1996, Jack Neufield, "Democracy"

LIFE: May 22, 1964, Shana Alexander, "A Born Loser's Success and Precarious Love"

LIFE: March 18, 1966, Diana Lurie, "They All Come Thinking I Can't Be That Great"

LIFE: February 14, 1969, John Gregory Dunne (from *The Studio,* Farrar, Straus & Giroux, 1969), "Dolly's Dilemma"

LIFE: January 9, 1970, Barbra Streisand, "Who Am I Anyway?"

LIFE: December 1983, Anne Fadiman, "Barbra Puts Her Career on the Line with *Yentl*"

London Express, April 19, 1966, Herbert Kretzmer

Look: April 5, 1966, Thomas Morgan, "Superbarbra"

Look: October 15, 1968, Ira Mother

Newsweek: January 5, 1970, Joseph Morgenstern, "Superstar—the Streisand Story"

Newsweek: November 28, 1983, Jack Kroll

New Times Magazine: January 24, 1975, Marie Brenner, "Barbra Streisand: A Star Is Shorn"

New West: November 22, 1976, Frank Pierson, "My Battles with Barbra and Jon"

New Yorker: November 14, 1970, Pauline Kael

New Yorker: December 30, 1972, Pauline Kael

New Yorker: March 17, 1975, Pauline Kael

New Yorker: June 20, 1994, Whitney Balliett

New York Observer, December 2004, Andrew Sarris

New York Post: June 22, 1994, Liz Smith

New York Times: June 18, 1970, Vincent Canby

New York Times: November 4, 1970, Vincent Canby

New York Times: November 10, 1985, Stephen Holden

New York Times: April 3, 1994, William Grimes

New York Times: June 22, 1994, Jon Pareles

New York Times: November 13, 1996, Bernard Weinraub

New York Times: April 10, 2001

New York Times: September 30, 2002

New York Times: December 22, 2004, Manohla Dargis

People: December 12, 1983, Brad Darrach, "Celebration of a Father"

Playboy: October 1977, cover story *Playboy* interview by Lawrence Grobel

Premiere: Special Edition, 1993

Rolling Stone: Issue 99, 1971, Stephen Holden

Saturday Evening Post: July 27, 1963, Pete Hamill, "Good-Bye Brooklyn—Hello Fame"

Seventeen: October 1963, "Barbra Streisand: Singing, Swinging Show-Stopper!"

Time: April 10, 1964, Ray Kennedy, "The Girl"

Time: March 21, 1975, Jay Cocks

US: October 9, 2000, Todd Gold, "Barbra Streisand—The Farewell Interview"

Vanity Fair: November 1991, Kevin Sessums, "Streisand Now"

Vanity Fair: November 1994, Michael Shnayerson, "A Star Is Reborn"

Variety: April 21, 1995

Variety: April 8, 1996

Village Voice: March 14, 1975, Molly Haskell

Washington Post: December 15, 1991

Woman: November 5, 1978

Index